# Better Homes and Gardens ®

# ENCYCLOPEDIA
## of
# COOKING

*Volume 5*

Delectable Apricot-Coconut Ring rates high with coconut fans.
Cake mix bakes in ring mold atop brown sugar-coconut glaze.
To serve, spoon glaze over apricots mounded in cake ring.

**On the cover:** Golden harvest corn is studded with plump,
tender kernels. A versatile vegetable, corn appeals to all ages
whether served on-the-cob or added to soups or casseroles.

# BETTER HOMES AND GARDENS BOOKS
## NEW YORK • DES MOINES

© Meredith Corporation, 1970, 1971, 1973. All Rights Reserved.
Printed in the United States of America.
Special Edition. Second Printing, 1973.
Library of Congress Catalog Card Number: 73-83173
SBN: 696-02025-4

**CHOCOLATE CHIP**—One of the names given to a semisweet chocolate piece that is small, and uniformly sized and shaped.

## Chocolate Cheese Pie

*Please both cheesecake fans and chocolate fans with one elegant dessert—*

1½ cups fine graham cracker crumbs
½ cup butter or margarine, melted

. . .

1 6-ounce package semisweet chocolate pieces (1 cup)
2 3-ounce packages cream cheese, softened
½ cup sugar
1 teaspoon vanilla
¼ teaspoon salt
2 egg yolks

. . .

1 cup whipping cream
2 egg whites
¼ cup sugar

Mix cracker crumbs and melted butter or margarine; press into a 9-inch pie plate. Chill.

Melt chocolate pieces over hot, *not boiling*, water. Cool slightly. Blend cream cheese, ½ cup sugar, vanilla, and salt. Add egg yolks, one at a time, beating well after each. Stir in melted chocolate; chill till thick. Beat smooth.

Whip cream; fold cream into chocolate. Beat egg whites to soft peaks. Gradually add ¼ cup sugar, beating till stiff peaks form; fold into chocolate. Pile into crust. Place in freezer till well chilled; remove 5 to 10 minutes before serving. Makes 8 servings.

**CHOCOLATE DAIRY DRINK**—A dairy-produced beverage made of skimmed milk or partially skimmed milk, flavored with chocolate syrup or cocoa and sweetened. An 8-ounce glass contains about 190 calories.

**CHOCOLATE DECORATIVE CANDY**—The name given to uniformly shaped ⅛- to ¼-inch long slender pieces of semisweet chocolate used for decorating cakes, cookies, or other desserts. They retain their shape during baking at moderate temperatures.

Create a luscious sundae with chocolate and vanilla ice cream. Then spoon Easy Chocolate Sauce and walnuts over the top.

**CHOCOLATE MILK**—A beverage made of whole milk flavored with chocolate syrup or powder and sweetened. An 8-ounce glass of chocolate milk contains about 213 calories. Cold chocolate milk is a delightful drink as is, or can be heated and used as the base for other beverages.

## Spiced Chocolate Coffee

*A simple and jiffy recipe to prepare—*

2 tablespoons instant coffee powder
Dash ground cinnamon
1 cup water
2 cups chocolate milk
Sweetened whipped cream

Combine coffee powder and cinnamon in small saucepan. Stir in water and chocolate milk. Heat, stirring constantly, till piping hot. Pour into small cups and put a spoonful of sweetened whipped cream atop each serving. Makes six ½-cup servings.

**CHOCOLATE SAUCE**—A dessert sauce that can be prepared at home or purchased at the store. Chocolate or cocoa and sugar are the basic ingredients, with milk or cream as the liquid, and corn syrup or butter as possible additions. Other flavorings are occasionally added. You might enjoy flavor blends such as chocolate-mint, chocolate-carmel, or others found in the store.

## Easy Chocolate Sauce

In small heavy saucepan heat one 6-ounce package semisweet chocolate pieces (1 cup) and ½ cup evaporated milk over medium heat, stirring constantly till blended. Serve warm or at room temperature. Makes 1 cup.

## Regal Chocolate Sauce

½ cup light corn syrup
1 cup sugar
3 1-ounce squares unsweetened chocolate, broken up
1 teaspoon vanilla
½ cup evaporated milk

Chocolate syrup (right) and sauce (left) are closely related except chocolate sauce has milk, cream, and/or butter added.

Combine corn syrup, sugar, and 1 cup water in saucepan. Cook to soft-ball stage (236°). Remove from heat. Add chocolate; stir till melted. Add vanilla. Slowly add evaporated milk; mix thoroughly. Cool. Makes 1¾ cups.

**CHOCOLATE SYRUP**—A thin chocolate- or cocoa-flavored syrup made with sugar, water, salt, and other flavorings. The syrup is often used as the flavor base for making beverages, frozen desserts, or ice cream sodas, and can be used as an ice cream topper. Chocolate syrup is available in jars and cans at supermarkets, or it can be prepared at home.

## Chocolate Syrup

½ cup sugar
¼ cup unsweetened cocoa powder
    Dash salt
½ cup water
1 teaspoon vanilla

Mix sugar, cocoa powder, and salt in saucepan. Add water. Bring to boiling. Reduce heat and cook 1 minute. Remove from heat and add vanilla. Cool. Store in refrigerator. Makes ⅔ cup. (For a quick beverage, combine 2 tablespoons syrup and 1 cup milk. Heat. Serves 1.)

## Brazilian Chocolate

*A good breakfast beverage—*

½ cup chocolate syrup
¼ teaspoon salt
¼ teaspoon ground cinnamon
2 tablespoons instant coffee powder
2 cups hot water
2 cups hot milk
1 teaspoon vanilla

In saucepan combine syrup, salt, cinnamon, and coffee powder. Stir in ¼ *cup* of the water; cook over medium-low heat till heated through. Add remaining water and milk. Cook just till heated through, stirring occasionally. Add vanilla; beat with rotary beater till foamy. Serve immediately. Makes 6 servings.

A cross-bladed, rocker-type chopper and a small wooden bowl make chopping a small quantity of nuts quick and easy.

Chop with a French chef's knife. Place fingertips on top of blade near point. Rock knife up and down, pivoting on point.

**CHOKECHERRY**—The fruit of a wild cherry tree native to North America. The fruit is sharp in flavor and is best used in jelly or jam to be served on slices of toast.

**CHOLESTEROL**—A fatlike substance present in all animal cells and an essential component of the blood and other parts of the body. Manufactured by the liver and other organs, cholesterol regulates the passage of substances through the cell walls of the body.

Cholesterol is present in meat fat, egg yolks, liver, brains, kidneys, shellfish, and dairy fats. The body's cholesterol level and types of fat consumed are being studied in the search for causes of hardening of the arteries and heart disease. Results of these investigations, however, are incomplete.

**CHOP**—1. The motion of cutting food with a knife, chopper, or blender into small pieces about the size of peas. 2. Individual cuts of meat from the loin or rib areas, consisting of bone and tender muscle. It usually refers to lamb, veal, or pork.

**CHOP SUEY**—A main dish with an Oriental name and ingredients, but of American origin. It may include pieces of pork or poultry, bean sprouts, bamboo shoots, water chestnuts, soy sauce, and mushrooms, and is served with rice. Chop suey is also available as a canned or frozen product. (See also *Oriental Cookery.*)

## Turkey Chop Suey

½ cup sliced onion
2 tablespoons butter or margarine
2 cups diced cooked turkey
2 cups chicken broth
1 cup sliced celery
1 5-ounce can water chestnuts, drained and thinly sliced
3 tablespoons soy sauce
¼ cup cornstarch
1 16-ounce can bean sprouts

In saucepan cook onion in butter till tender but not brown. Add turkey, broth, celery, and water chestnuts; heat to boiling. Combine ⅓ cup water, soy sauce, and cornstarch; stir into turkey mixture. Cook and stir till mixture is thickened and bubbly.

Drain bean sprouts; add to mixture and heat through. Serve on hot rice sprinkled with toasted slivered almonds, if desired. Pass additional soy sauce. Makes 4 to 6 servings.

**CHORIZO**—A hot and peppery Spanish or Mexican pork sausage. (See also *Sausage.*)

**CHOU PASTE, CHOUX PASTE**—The French puff pastry dough from which cream puffs and éclairs are made. The round cream puff itself is known as a chou.

**CHOW CHOW**—A sweet pickle relish of chopped mixed vegetables strongly flavored with mustard. Both mustard seed and dry mustard may be used. The name originally referred to a Chinese relish of orange peel and ginger in a sweet syrup.

## Chow Chow

        7 **large onions (4 cups)**
        1 **medium head cabbage (4 cups)**
      10 **green tomatoes (4 cups)**
      12 **green peppers (5 cups)**
        6 **sweet red peppers (1½ cups)**
      ½ **cup granulated pickling salt**
        6 **cups sugar**
        2 **tablespoons mustard seed**
        1 **tablespoon celery seed**
    1½ **teaspoons turmeric**
        4 **cups cider vinegar**

Wash vegetables. Using coarse blade, grind onions, cabbage, green tomatoes, and peppers. Sprinkle with pickling salt; let mixture stand overnight. Rinse and drain.

Combine sugar, mustard seed, celery seed, turmeric, vinegar, and 2 cups water. Pour over vegetables. Bring to boil; boil gently 5 minutes.

Fill hot jars to within ½ inch of tops; adjust lids. Process jars in boiling water bath 5 minutes (start timing when the water returns to a full boil). Makes 9 pints.

**CHOWDER**—A thick soup, usually milk-based, and generally made with fish or shellfish. Chowder frequently contains bacon or salt pork and diced potatoes, while other vegetables may be included.

Chowder is said to have originated many years ago when French sailors, shipwrecked off the coast of New England, concocted a stew using the foods they had managed to salvage and clams dug from the sandy shore. The big iron kettle in which the stew was cooked was called a *chaudière*. It is easy to see how the Americanized name came into being.

Variations in chowder preparation have led to many arguments. New Englanders claim that fish or clam chowder is always made with milk as the base, salt pork as the fat, and diced potatoes as the thickener. Manhattan-style chowder, scorned in New England, contains tomatoes and other vegetables in a clear broth. In those parts of the country where fresh seafood is not readily available, the term chowder applies to a thick, creamy soup made with corn, potatoes, chicken, or cheese.

Whatever the ingredients, chowder is a meal in a bowl. Assorted crisp crackers and an easy fruit dessert complete a menu to nourish and satisfy. (See also *Soup*.)

## New England Clam Chowder

        2 **dozen medium-size quahog clams**
            *or* **2 7½-ounce cans clams**
            *or* **1 pint fresh shucked clams**
      ¼ **pound salt pork, minced**
    1½ **cups water**
        4 **cups diced, peeled potatoes**
      ½ **cup chopped onion**
        2 **cups milk**
        1 **cup light cream**
        3 **tablespoons all-purpose flour**
    1½ **teaspoons salt**
           **Dash pepper**

If using clams in shell, place them in large kettle; add 1 cup water. Cover and bring to boiling. Reduce heat; steam just till shells open, 5 to 10 minutes. Remove clams from shells.

Dice clams, reserving ½ cup clam liquor. Fry minced salt pork till crisp. Remove bits of pork; reserve. Add ½ cup clam liquor, water, potatoes, and onion to fat. Cook covered till potatoes are tender, 15 to 20 minutes.

Add clams, 1¾ *cups* milk, and the light cream. Blend remaining ¼ cup milk and flour; stir into chowder. Heat to boil; stir occasionally. Add seasonings and salt pork. Serves 6.

## *Seafood chowder by the bowlful*

New Englanders claim chowder must be →
seafood in a creamy soup, flavored with salt pork, and thickened with diced potatoes.

## Manhattan Clam Chowder

2 dozen medium-size quahog clams
  *or* 2 7½-ounce cans clams
  *or* 1 pint fresh shucked clams
3 slices bacon, finely diced
1 cup finely diced celery
1 cup chopped onion
1 16-ounce can tomatoes, cut up
2 cups diced, peeled potatoes
1 cup finely diced carrots
1½ teaspoons salt
¼ teaspoon dried thyme, crushed
  Dash pepper
2 tablespoons all-purpose flour
2 tablespoons water

If using clams in shell, place them in large kettle; add 1 cup water. Cover and bring to boiling. Reduce heat; steam just till shells open, 5 to 10 minutes. Remove clams from shells.

Dice clams finely. Strain liquor; reserve ½ cup. Partially cook bacon. Add celery and onion; cook till tender. Add 3 cups water and clam liquor. Add remaining vegetables and seasonings. Cover; simmer about 35 minutes. Blend flour with the 2 tablespoons cold water. Stir into chowder; cook and stir to boiling. Add clams; heat. Makes 6 to 8 servings.

## Clam Chowder au Vin

2 cups diced, peeled potato
½ cup chopped onion
½ cup chopped celery
¼ teaspoon salt
1 cup water
1 10¾-ounce can condensed
  Manhattan-style clam chowder
1 cup milk
1 7½-ounce can minced clams,
  drained
3 tablespoons dry white wine
½ cup whipping cream
2 tablespoons snipped parsley

In large saucepan combine potatoes, onion, celery, salt, and water. Cook covered, till potatoes are tender, about 10 minutes; mash slightly. Add chowder, milk, clams, and wine. Heat but *do not boil.* Whip cream; stir into chowder. Season with salt and pepper. Sprinkle with parsley. Makes 4 servings.

## Seafood Chowder

*Inlanders can enjoy full-bodied chowder by using frozen fish fillets of haddock, cod, or halibut—*

2 pounds fresh *or* frozen fish
  fillets (haddock, cod, etc.)*
¼ pound salt pork, diced
1 cup chopped onion
6 medium potatoes, peeled and
  cubed (about 4 cups)
2 cups water
2 teaspoons salt
¼ teaspoon pepper
2 cups milk
1 14½-ounce can evaporated
  milk (1⅔ cups)
2 tablespoons all-purpose flour

Thaw frozen fillets. In large saucepan cook diced salt pork slowly till golden brown. Drain, reserving 1 tablespoon fat. Set aside cooked pork. Return the 1 tablespoon fat to saucepan. Add onion; cook till tender but not brown. Add potatoes and water. Add fillets; sprinkle with salt and pepper. Bring to boiling; cook over low heat till potatoes are tender and fish flakes easily when tested with fork. This will take 15 to 20 minutes.

With slotted spatula, remove fish. Break fish into bite-size pieces; return to saucepan. Combine milk and evaporated milk; gradually stir into flour till smooth; add to fish mixture. Add cooked salt pork and cook over low heat till mixture is heated through but do not allow chowder to boil. Makes 8 servings.

*Or* use 2 pounds halibut steaks; remove skin and bones carefully before breaking into pieces.

## Cheese Chowder

*Vegetable and cheese in a main dish soup—*

Cook ¼ cup finely chopped onion in 2 tablespoons butter or margarine till tender. Blend in ¼ cup all-purpose flour. Add 2 cups milk; one 13¾-ounce can chicken broth (1¾ cups, not condensed); ¼ cup *each* finely diced carrot and finely diced celery; and dash *each* salt and paprika. Cook and stir till thickened and bubbly. Reduce heat; add ½ cup cubed sharp process American cheese. Stir to melt cheese. Simmer 15 minutes. Makes 4 servings.

## Corned Beef Chowder

*Corned beef and "little" cabbages in creamy base—*

1 10½-ounce can condensed cream
    of potato soup
3 cups milk
1 10-ounce package frozen Brussels
    sprouts, thawed and cut up
    Dash pepper
1 12-ounce can corned beef,
    broken into pieces

In a large saucepan blend soup and *half* of the milk. Stir in Brussels sprouts and pepper. Bring to boiling, stirring occasionally. Reduce heat; simmer till sprouts are tender, 15 minutes. Add remaining milk and beef. Heat. Serves 4 or 5.

## Corn Chowder

5 slices bacon
2 cups diced potato
1 cup onion slices
1 16-ounce can whole kernel
    corn, undrained
1 10½-ounce can condensed cream
    of mushroom soup
2 cups milk
1 teaspoon salt
    Dash pepper
2 tablespoons all-purpose flour

Crisp-cook bacon; crumble. Reserve 2 table-spoons drippings. Cook potatoes and onion in 1 cup boiling salted water till tender. Do not drain. Stir in corn, mushroom soup, milk, salt, and pepper. Blend flour with reserved bacon drippings; add to soup mixture. Cook and stir till thick. Simmer 5 minutes. Stir often. Top with crumbled bacon. Serves 6 to 8.

**CHOW MEIN**—1. The Chinese term for fried noodles. 2. A stir-fried main dish consisting of meat and crisp vegetables served with fried noodles. Unlike American chow mein noodles, the Chinese versions are thin egg noodles cooked in water, then fried quickly. Often they are made into nestlike cakes and fried till brown and slightly crisp on the outside but still soft inside. (See also *Oriental Cookery*.)

## Pork Chow Mein

1 pound pork, cut in *thin* strips
3 tablespoons salad oil
3 cups thin, bias-cut celery
    slices
1 cup sliced onion
1 6-ounce can sliced mushrooms,
    drained
3 tablespoons cornstarch
1 10½-ounce can condensed beef
    broth
¼ cup soy sauce
1 16-ounce can bean sprouts,
    drained
1 5-ounce can water chestnuts,
    drained and sliced
    Cooked thin egg noodles* *or*
    heated chow mein noodles

Cook pork in *1 tablespoon* oil till done, about 10 minutes. Set aside. Cook celery, onion, and mushrooms in remaining oil till crisp-tender; stir often. Blend cornstarch and ¼ cup cold water; add broth and soy sauce. Stir into vegetables. Add meat, bean sprouts, and water chestnuts. Cook and stir till thick and bubbly. Serve over noodles. Serves 4 or 5.
*If desired, fry in small batches in 1 tablespoon oil over high heat until slightly crisp.

**CHOW MEIN NOODLES**—Crisp, fried noodles primarily served with chow mein in America, but also used as a crunchy topper for casseroles. When seasoned and toasted, the noodles make a tasty snack.

## Noodle Nibbles

3 tablespoons melted butter or
    margarine
2 teaspoons soy sauce
4 drops bottled hot pepper sauce
1 3-ounce can chow mein noodles
¼ teaspoon celery salt
    Dash onion powder

Combine melted butter or margarine, soy sauce, and hot pepper sauce; drizzle over noodles. Toss lightly. Sprinkle with celery salt and onion powder; toss. Spread on jelly-roll pan. Toast at 275° for 12 to 15 minutes. Makes 2½ cups.

# CHRISTMAS

*Food for holiday feasting and gift giving and the hospitality associated with the season.*

Fellowship and sharing of food keynote Christmas celebrations around the world. The religious and spiritual significance of this Christian holiday shines throughout the season and is enhanced by foods and customs which have become an important part of family observances. For many this significance is based on the heritage of a particular nationality or tradition.

In most homes Christmas celebrations last more than one day. Preparations often begin in late November or early December when fruitcakes are baked and the fragrance of freshly baked cookies fills the air. In many countries the holiday extends from Christmas Eve until January 6—the Twelve Days of Christmas.

In Sweden the celebration starts on December 13, Saint Lucia's Day. A daughter of the house, dressed in white and wearing a crown of lighted candles, begins the day by taking special bread or buns and coffee to her parents and other family members before they rise. In some towns the Lucia girl also visits the needy. Friends and neighbors exchange visits and hospitality during the day.

Many of the foods of the season originated in England. It was during Henry VIII's reign that fruitcakes and plum puddings were first served. By the seventeenth century mincemeat was being used in Christmas pie. Some of these were huge, weighing up to 100 pounds with a box-shaped crust to represent the manger of the Christ Child. Spices and fruits used in pies and puddings were considered reminders of the gifts of the Magi.

The custom of having a nativity scene in the home began in Italy. St. Francis of Assisi celebrated Mass in the forest, while, nearby, real people and live animals depicted the nativity. The idea of repeating the setting in miniature spread and much of the house-to-house calling on friends includes viewing the crèche and sampling a rich, sweet holiday bread, filled with fruit and decorated with almonds.

In Mexico, the *posada,* a reenactment of Mary and Joseph's search for lodging, combines spiritual devotion, hospitality, and a treat for the children. Families form a procession to the homes of friends. Their symbolic admittance is climaxed when the children, blindfolded, break the piñata, a decorated clay or paper-mache container filled with candy and trinkets.

In some German traditions, Belsnickel, a cranky character, watches children to make sure they are good every day until Christmas. If a child has been on his best behavior all day, he is rewarded the next morning by finding a little plate with a Christmas cookie placed on an outside kitchen window sill. If he's been naughty, the plate might be empty or contain a stone instead of a cookie.

## Yuletide entertaining

Holiday parties take many forms, but food is always an important element. An open house is perhaps the easiest way to entertain. Friends come by to exchange the season's greetings and sample an array of goodies presented for their enjoyment. Most of the foods are made in advance to free the hostess at serving time.

*Sweets to say season's greetings*

← Jewel-topped Holiday Divinity and crunchy Peanut Brittle join Java Fudge and Peanut Butter Fudge as gifts from the kitchen.

The beverages offered at an open house are usually coffee, tea, and a cheery punch or Christmas beverage such as egg nog. All of these go well with fruitcake, cookies, and fancy breads. A hot punch is popular in cold climates. The Wassail bowl of Old English origin contains hot spiced fruit juice with or without wine. Glogg, another heated fruit and wine combination, comes from Scandinavia. Mixed drinks may be served, if desired.

## Rosy Wassail

In a large kettle combine 2 cups cranberry juice cocktail; one 6-ounce can frozen orange juice concentrate, thawed; 2 cups water; 1 table-spoon sugar; and ¼ teaspoon allspice. Bring *almost* to simmering. Add 3¼ cups dry sauterne; heat through, but do not boil. If desired, stir in a few drops red food coloring. Stud thick orange slices with whole cloves. Pour punch into preheated punch bowl; float orange slices atop. Makes 12 to 14 servings.

## Cranberry-Cherry Punch

Dissolve one 3-ounce package cherry-flavored gelatin in 1 cup boiling water. Stir in one 6-ounce can frozen lemonade concentrate. Add 3 cups cold water and one chilled 1-quart bottle cranberry juice cocktail. Pour over ice in punch bowl. Resting bottle on rim of bowl, slowly pour one chilled 28-ounce bottle ginger ale down the side; mix with up-and-down motion. Garnish with lime slices. Makes 25 servings.

Christmas dinner is one of the truly festive meals of the year. When the family gathering is large, roast turkey or goose, or perhaps a glazed ham, will provide ample servings. Smaller families might borrow from a Danish menu by serving Roast Duckling with Red Cabbage.

Accompaniments add a bountiful note to the dinner. Star-shaped molded salads are popular because they suit the season and can be made well ahead of time. If one or two kinds of potatoes plus a cooked vegetable—perhaps some buttered squash, creamed onions, or green beans amandine

---

## ❋MENU❋

### HOLIDAY FEAST

*Herring in Sour Cream*
*Roast Duckling*
*Red Cabbage    Parsley Buttered Potatoes*
*Cranberry-sauced Peaches*
*Hard Rolls    Celery and Carrot Sticks*
*Fruitcake*
*Beverage*

---

—are part of the menu, some hostesses prefer to pass a giant relish tray or crisp vegetables and pickles instead of a salad.

In some families plum pudding is a must for dessert. Others prefer mince pie, fruitcake, or a choice of cookies.

## Roast Duckling with Red Cabbage

    2 ducklings, 3 to 5 pounds each
    6 cups shredded red cabbage
 ¼  cup currant jelly
    2 tablespoons butter or margarine
    1 tablespoon vinegar
 ¾  teaspoon caraway seed
 ½  teaspoon salt

Prick skin of ducklings; place on rack in shallow roasting pan. Roast, uncovered, at 375° for 1½ to 2 hours. Increase temperature to 425°; roast an additional 15 minutes.

In large saucepan or kettle cook cabbage in boiling, salted water till tender, 10 minutes; drain well. Return to saucepan. In small saucepan combine remaining ingredients. Heat and stir till butter is melted. Pour over cabbage; toss and stir till cabbage is heated through. Serve with ducklings. Makes 4 to 5 servings.

### *Borrow a menu from Scandinavia*

Follow a Danish theme by serving Roast → Duckling with Red Cabbage. It is a festive choice for a small family gathering.

```
┌─────────────────────────────────┐
│         ❖MENU❖                  │
│                                 │
│      CHRISTMAS  DINNER          │
│          Fruit Cup              │
│      Currant Glazed Ham         │
│  Mashed Sweet Potatoes  Onions Au Gratin │
│      Molded Ruby Red Salad      │
│  Cloverleaf Rolls      Relish Tray │
│       Mincemeat Cake            │
│          Beverage               │
└─────────────────────────────────┘
```

## Currant-Glazed Ham

  14- to 16-pound fully cooked ham
      Whole cloves
  ¾ cup currant jelly
  ½ cup dark corn syrup
  ¼ teaspoon prepared horseradish
  ⅛ teaspoon dry mustard

Place ham, fat side up, on rack in shallow pan; insert meat thermometer. Heat at 325° till thermometer registers 130°, about 3 hours. About 30 minutes before ham is done, remove from oven; score diagonally, if desired. Stud with cloves. Return to oven; baste often with *Currant Glaze:* In saucepan combine jelly, corn syrup, horseradish, and dry mustard. Cook and stir over medium-low heat till blended.

## Molded Ruby Red Salad

*Avocado slices form a holiday wreath inside—*

Heat 2 cups cranberry-juice cocktail to boiling. Add two 3-ounce packages raspberry-flavored gelatin; stir to dissolve. Add one 8¾-ounce can pineapple tidbits, undrained; ½ cup port; and ½ cup water. Peel and slice 1 avocado; arrange slices in bottom of 5½-cup mold.

Pour enough gelatin mixture over avocado to cover; chill till almost set. Chill remaining cranberry mixture till partially set; fold in 1 cup diced peeled apple and ½ cup finely chopped celery. Pour over avocado layer. Chill till firm. Unmold. Makes 8 to 10 servings.

# Festive breads

Among the joys of Christmas baking are the rich breads fragrant with spices and studded with bright bits of candied fruit or plump raisins. Before baking, the dough is braided or formed into special shapes befitting the season. While still warm from the oven, frosting is drizzled over the golden brown crust. Nuts, cherries, or colored sugars are used as trimmings.

## Lucia Braid

  2 packages active dry yeast
  5 to 5⅓ cups sifted all-purpose
      flour
  ½ teaspoon ground cardamom
  1⅓ cups milk
  ½ cup sugar
  ½ cup shortening
  1½ teaspoons salt
  2 eggs
      Confectioners' sugar glaze
      Walnut halves
      Red and green candied cherries

In large mixer bowl combine yeast, *3 cups* of the flour, and cardamom. Heat milk, sugar, shortening, and salt till warm; stir to melt shortening. Add to dry mixture in mixing bowl; add egg. Beat at low speed with electric mixer for ½ minute, scraping sides of bowl constantly. Beat 3 minutes at high speed. By hand, stir in enough of the flour to make a soft dough.

Turn dough out on well-floured surface. Knead till smooth and elastic, about 8 to 10 minutes. Place dough in lightly greased bowl; turning once to grease the surface. Cover, let rise in a warm place till doubled, about 2 hours. Punch down. Divide dough in half; cover and let rest 10 minutes. Divide each half in 4 parts.

Roll 3 parts of dough in 20-inch strands; braid. Carefully place braid around a greased, 6-ounce juice can standing upright on a greased baking sheet. Seal ends of dough together to form continuous braid. Divide 4th part of dough in half. Shape in two 20-inch strands and twist together. Place on top of large braid. Make second coffee cake with remaining pieces.

Let rise in warm place till doubled, about 1 hour. Bake at 350° till golden brown, about 25 minutes. Remove juice can.

While braids are still warm, brush with Confectioners' Sugar Glaze. Decorate tops with nuts and candied cherries. Makes 2 coffee cakes.

*Confectioners' Sugar Glaze:* Add enough milk or cream to 2 cups sifted confectioners' sugar to make it spreading consistency. Add 1 teaspoon vanilla and dash salt; mix well.

### Jewel-Top Star Mold

*Trim bakes in pan like an upside-down cake—*

```
  1   package active dry yeast
 1/4  cup milk
  3   tablespoons shortening
  3   tablespoons granulated sugar
  1   teaspoon grated lemon peel
 1/2  teaspoon salt
  1   egg
1 1/2 cups sifted all-purpose flour
            . . .
  1   tablespoon butter or margarine,
        melted
  2   tablespoons brown sugar
  1   tablespoon light corn syrup
      Candied pineapple
      Candied cherries
```

Soften dry yeast in 1/4 cup warm water. Heat milk and shortening till shortening melts; cool to lukewarm. Pour into mixing bowl. Stir in granulated sugar, lemon peel, and salt. Add egg and softened yeast. Add flour, 1/2 cup at a time, beating smooth after each addition. Cover and let rise till double. Stir down dough. Combine butter, brown sugar, and corn syrup; spread on bottom of 5 1/2-cup star mold. Arrange fruit in mold to form pattern. Spoon dough carefully over fruit. Cover and let rise till double. Bake at 375° for 20 to 25 minutes. Cool 1 minute. Loosen sides and turn out onto rack. Cool.

Giving away holiday breads is part of the fun of baking. Sturdy cardboard, cut to fit and slipped under the bread, will support your gift as you carry it to a neighbor or friend. A new bread board or baking sheet tucked under the loaf also can be a part of the gift. Clear plastic wrap used as a covering material serves two purposes. It lets the gaily-decorated loaf show through as it protects the bread.

# Gift-worthy candies

An assortment of Christmas candies makes a dandy holiday remembrance. Show off your talents as a candymaker by offering candies with a variety of interesting textures and flavors. A good selection should include some that contain combinations of nuts, fruit, or coconut and others that are plain. In peanut brittles or other nut brittles, the nuts are essential both for flavor and crunch. But, in many candies the ingredients can be mixed or matched to suit your fancy.

Velvety-smooth chocolate fudge is an all-time favorite, but this year why not treat your friends to Java Fudge or Peanut Butter Fudge. Let taffy or caramels provide a delightful contrast in chewiness. Creamy white divinity can be dressed up with candied-fruit jewels.

The container for these masterpieces may be as simple as a brightly papered box, or as fancy as a candy dish or brandy snifter tied with a saucy red bow.

### Peanut Butter Fudge

In a large, warm bowl combine 1 pint marshmallow creme, 1 cup chunk-style peanut butter, and 1 teaspoon vanilla. In a heavy saucepan combine 2 cups sugar and 2/3 cup milk. Cook sugar mixture to soft ball stage, or till candy thermometer registers 234°. Pour over peanut butter mixture. Blend well. Spread in buttered 8- or 9-inch square pan. Cool; cut in squares.

### Java Fudge

In heavy 3-quart saucepan combine 3 cups sugar, 4 teaspoons instant coffee powder, and dash salt. Stir in 1 cup milk, 1/2 cup light cream, and 2 tablespoons light corn syrup. Bring to boiling stirring constantly. Continue boiling over medium heat without stirring, till candy thermometer registers 234°. Remove from heat; add 3 tablespoons butter or margarine and 1 teaspoon vanilla. *Do not stir.* Cool to 110°.

Beat till mixture begins to thicken and starts to lose its gloss. Quickly stir in 1/4 cup chopped walnuts. Pour into buttered 8-inch pan. Cool; cut into squares. Makes 1 1/2 pounds.

## Molasses Taffy

Butter sides of heavy 2-quart saucepan. In it combine 2 cups granulated sugar, 1 cup light molasses, and ⅓ cup water. Heat slowly stirring constantly till sugar dissolves. Bring mixture to boiling; add 2 teaspoons vinegar. Cook to soft-crack stage (268°).

Remove from heat; add 2 tablespoons butter. Sift in ½ teaspoon soda; stir to mix. Pour into buttered 15½x10½x1-inch pan. Cool till comfortable to handle. Butter hands; gather taffy into ball and pull with fingertips. When light taffy color and hard to pull, cut into fourths. Pull each piece into long strand about ½ inch thick. With buttered scissors cut in bite-size pieces; wrap in waxed paper. Makes 1¼ pounds.

## Peanut Brittle

>     2 cups sugar
>     1 cup light corn syrup
>     1 cup water
>     2 cups raw Spanish or Virginia*
>         peanuts
>     ½ teaspoon salt
>     1 teaspoon butter or margarine
>     ½ teaspoon soda

Combine sugar, syrup, and water in heavy skillet. Cook slowly, stirring till sugar dissolves. Cook to soft-ball stage (234°). Add peanuts and salt. Cook to hard-crack stage (290°), stirring constantly. (Remove candy from heat while testing.) Add butter and soda; stir quickly to blend. (Mixture will bubble.) Pour at once onto 2 well-buttered 15½x10½x1-inch jelly roll pans. Tilt pans slightly to allow candy to spread in thin layer. Break in pieces when cold. Makes about 1½ pounds candy.

*Blanch peanuts in boiling water. Let stand 3 minutes; run under cold water; peel.

### *Pass Christmas cookies and cake*

←Decorated Family-Style Sugar Cookies and Gingerbreadmen, Chocolate Spritz, Orange-Date Bars, and Mint-Topped Brownies join Cranberry-Cherry Punch and triple-layered Mincemeat Cake as holiday refreshments. (See *Gingerbread* for Gingerbreadmen.)

## Holiday Divinity

>     ½ cup light corn syrup
>     2½ cups sugar
>     ¼ teaspoon salt
>     ½ cup water
>     2 egg whites
>     1 teaspoon vanilla
>     1 cup coarsely chopped walnuts
>     ¼ cup chopped candied cherries
>     ¼ cup chopped candied pineapple

In saucepan mix corn syrup, sugar, salt, and water. Cook, stirring, till sugar is dissolved. Continue cooking, without stirring, till candy thermometer registers 248° or till firm-ball stage. Beat egg whites till stiff peaks form. Gradually pour about *half* the syrup over whites, beating constantly with electric mixer. Then cook remainder of syrup till thermometer registers 272° or till soft-crack stage. Slowly beat into first mixture. Add vanilla. Beat till mixture holds its shape. If necessary, allow mixture to stand about 5 minutes to stiffen; stir occasionally. Add nuts and fruits. Drop by teaspoonfuls onto waxed paper. Makes 4 dozen.

# Cookies with trimmings

Cookie baking for the holidays is a labor of love. Soft bars, crisp rolled cookies, and tender spritz head the list of favorites. Frostings and trims add to the fun especially when the children help.

Sugar cookies are perhaps the most versatile because each shape and decoration yields a different looking cookie. Use fancy cutters, or make your own pattern out of heavy paper and trace the design onto the rolled dough. To turn sugar cookies into Christmas ornaments, simply make a tiny hole near the top of each cookie before it goes into the oven. The point of a skewer or wooden pick will do the job nicely. When baked, the opening is just right for stringing the ornament with twine or yarn.

Many cookies that are filled with candied fruit and spices stay moist throughout the season's entertaining if stored in tightly covered containers or frozen. Brandy Balls and Cherry-Almond Balls are good keepers—that is if hungry nibblers don't get into the cookie jar first.

## Family-Style Sugar Cookies

     2 cups sifted all-purpose flour
     ¾ cup sugar
     1 teaspoon baking powder
     ¼ teaspoon salt
       Dash nutmeg
     ½ cup shortening
     1 beaten egg
     ⅓ cup milk
     ½ teaspoon vanilla

Sift together flour, sugar, baking powder, salt, and nutmeg. Using pastry blender, cut in shortening till like fine crumbs. Combine egg, milk, and vanilla. Stir into flour-shortening mixture. Blend well. On floured surface roll to ⅛-inch thickness for crisp cookies or ¼-inch for softer cookies. Cut with cutters. Sprinkle with sugar *or* leave plain if cookies are to be frosted. Bake on lightly greased cookie sheets at 375° for 7 to 8 minutes for thin cookies and 11 to 12 minutes for thicker cookies. Makes 2 dozen cookies, ⅛ inch thick *or* 1½ dozen ¼ inch thick.

## Fruitcake Cookies

     ¼ cup butter or margarine
     ¾ cup brown sugar
     1 egg
     ¼ cup evaporated milk
     1 teaspoon lemon juice
           • • •
     1 cup sifted all-purpose flour
     ¼ teaspoon baking soda
     ¼ teaspoon salt
     ½ teaspoon ground cinnamon
     ½ teaspoon ground cloves
     ½ teaspoon ground allspice
       Dash ground nutmeg
     1 cup chopped mixed candied fruits
       and peels
     1 cup chopped pecans
     ¾ cup raisins

Cream butter and sugar till fluffy; beat in egg. Combine milk and lemon juice; gradually add to creamed mixture. Reserve ¼ cup flour. Sift remaining flour with soda, salt, and spices; stir into creamed mixture. Mix reserved flour with fruits and pecans; blend into dough. Drop by teaspoon on lightly greased cookie sheet. Bake at 375° for 10 to 12 minutes. Makes 60.

## Chocolate Spritz

     1½ cups butter or margarine
     1 cup sugar
     2 ounces unsweetened chocolate,
       melted
     1 egg
     1 teaspoon vanilla
     ½ teaspoon almond extract
     4 cups sifted all-purpose flour
     1 teaspoon baking powder

In large mixer bowl thoroughly cream butter and sugar; add melted chocolate, egg, vanilla, and almond extract. Beat well.

Sift together flour and baking powder. Add to creamed mixture; mix till smooth. Do not chill. Force dough through cookie press, forming various shapes, on greased cookie sheet. Bake at 400° 8 to 10 minutes. Cool. Decorate.

## Snowy Cinnamon Stars

Mix ⅔ cup sugar, 1 teaspoon ground cinnamon, and ½ teaspoon grated lemon peel. Beat 2 egg whites till soft peaks form. Gradually add sugar mixture. Beat till very stiff peaks form. Fold in 1¾ cups ground almonds. Chill.

On lightly floured surface, roll dough ⅛ inch thick. Cut with 2½-inch star cutter. Place on well-greased cookie sheet. Frost to points with Meringue. Trim with silver candies. Bake at 325° for 12 to 15 minutes; remove from sheet at once. Cool on rack. Makes about 3 dozen.

*Meringue:* Beat 1 egg white till soft peaks form. Gradually add 1 cup sifted confectioners' sugar, beating after each addition. Continue beating till stiff peaks form. Frost star cookies with meringue before baking.

## Date-Orange Bars

Cream ¼ cup butter and ½ cup brown sugar till fluffy. Add 1 egg and 1 teaspoon grated orange peel; beat well. Sift together 1 cup sifted all-purpose flour, ½ teaspoon baking powder, and ½ teaspoon soda; add to creamed mixture. Stir in ¼ cup milk, ¼ cup orange juice, ½ cup chopped walnuts, and ½ cup chopped dates.

Spread in greased 11x7x1½-inch pan. Bake at 350° for 25 minutes. Cool; sprinkle with confectioners' sugar. Makes 24.

## Brandy Balls

2½ cups finely crushed vanilla
    wafers (about 60 wafers)
1 cup sifted confectioners' sugar
2 tablespoons unsweetened cocoa
    powder
½ cup finely chopped walnuts
¼ cup brandy
¼ cup light corn syrup

Combine wafer crumbs, confectioners' sugar, cocoa powder, and nuts. Stir in brandy and corn syrup. Add a little water (about 1¼ teaspoons) if necessary to form mixture into ¾-inch balls. Roll in granulated sugar. Store in tightly covered container. Makes 4 dozen.

## Cherry-Almond Balls

¾ cup butter or margarine
⅓ cup sifted confectioners' sugar
1 teaspoon vanilla
¼ teaspoon salt
2 cups sifted all-purpose flour
½ cup finely chopped almonds
    Whole candied cherries (about
    60 cherries)

Cream together butter, sugar, vanilla, and salt till fluffy. Add flour and almonds; mix well. Wrap a teaspoonful of dough around each cherry. Place on baking sheet. Bake at 325° for 20 minutes. Cool slightly. Roll in sifted confectioners' sugar. Makes about 5 dozen.

## Mint-Frosted Brownies

Thoroughly cream ½ cup butter or margarine, 1 cup sugar, and 1 teaspoon vanilla. Add 2 eggs and beat well. Blend in 2 ounces unsweetened chocolate, melted. Stir in ½ cup sifted all-purpose flour and ½ cup chopped nuts. Bake in greased 8x8x2-inch pan at 350° for 30 to 35 minutes. Cool; frost with Mint Frosting.

*Mint Frosting:* Cream 3 tablespoons soft butter, ½ teaspoon peppermint extract, and dash salt. Gradually add 1 cup sifted confectioners' sugar, creaming till light and fluffy. Add 2 tablespoons milk or cream and another cup sifted confectioners' sugar. Beat till smooth. Tint with few drops red or green food coloring.

# Traditional desserts

Leading contenders in many countries for this title are fruitcake, plum pudding, or desserts made with mincemeat. Showy desserts such as a Lithuanian Strawberry Torte are favored, too.

Fruitcake takes special honors in the make-ahead category because many varieties can be baked several weeks in advance and stored to mellow before slicing. The fruitcake is wrapped in brandy-soaked cheesecloth and placed in a canister with a snug-fitting lid. If you prefer, wedges of apple changed periodically during storage may replace the moistened cheesecloth. Should you be tardy in baking your fruitcake, last-minute versions like this Whole Nut Fruitcake are delicious, too.

## Whole Nut Fruitcake

Sift together 1 cup sifted all-purpose flour, 1 teaspoon baking powder, and ⅛ teaspoon salt. Separate 4 eggs. Beat yolks till thick. Add 1 cup sugar to egg yolks, beating constantly. Add ¼ cup milk and sifted dry ingredients. Beat egg whites till stiff peaks form. Fold beaten egg whites into the batter.

In a large bowl, mix 16 ounces pitted dates with 8 ounces *each* candied pineapple, whole candied cherries, mixed candied fruit and peels, pecan halves, walnut halves, and whole Brazil nuts. Add batter and mix well. Spoon fruitcake mixture into two well-greased and floured 9x5x3-inch pans. Bake at 325° for 1½ hours. Cool; remove fruitcake from pans. When cold, store fruitcake in an airtight container.

Christmas plum pudding can be made ahead and reheated, but many hostesses will serve it steaming hot from the mold. For a spectacular touch, it may be served aflame. Warmed brandy, ignited and quickly poured over the pudding, will wreathe it in flame. Another way to flame the plum pudding is to saturate sugar cubes with brandy or lemon extract, arrange them around the base of the pudding and ignite the cubes. Flamed or not, hard sauce or foamy sauce are accompaniments to pass with this traditional dessert.

## English Plum Pudding

    1 cup all-purpose flour
    1 teaspoon baking soda
    1 teaspoon salt
    1 teaspoon ground cinnamon
    ¾ teaspoon ground mace
    ¼ teaspoon ground nutmeg
    8 ounces raisins (1½ cups)
    8 ounces currants (1½ cups)
    4 ounces mixed candied fruits
        and peels (½ cup)
    ½ cup chopped walnuts
    2 cups coarse soft bread
        crumbs (4 slices)
    4 ounces ground suet (1½ cups)
    1 cup brown sugar
    2 beaten eggs
    ¼ cup currant jelly
    ⅓ cup brandy
        Hard Sauce

Sift together flour, soda, salt, and spices. Stir in fruits, nuts, and bread crumbs. Combine suet, sugar, eggs, jelly, and brandy. Blend into flour-fruit mixture. Pour into two well-greased 1-quart molds; cover tightly. Steam 3 to 3½ hours. Let stand 5 to 10 minutes; unmold. Serve warm with Hard Sauce.

*Hard Sauce:* Thoroughly cream ½ cup butter with 2 cups sifted confectioners' sugar. Beat in 1 tablespoon brandy. Chill in mold or bowl; unmold before serving. *Or* use pastry tube to make individual decorations; chill till firm.

## Mincemeat Cake

Cream together 1½ cups sugar and ½ cup shortening. Add 3 eggs and 1 teaspoon vanilla; beat till fluffy. Sift together 2½ cups sifted all-purpose flour, 2 teaspoons baking powder, 1 teaspoon baking soda, and 1 teaspoon salt. Add alternately with 1 cup milk to sugar mixture, beating thoroughly after each addition. Fold in 1½ cups prepared mincemeat.

Divide batter evenly among 3 greased and floured 9-inch round cake pans. Bake at 350° for 25 to 30 minutes. Cool 10 minutes. Remove from pans and fill with Vanilla Nut Filling. Drizzle with a confectioners' sugar glaze.

*Vanilla Nut Filling:* Make one 3-ounce package regular vanilla pudding mix following label. Cool; stir in ¼ cup chopped pecans.

## Strawberry Torte

    1 cup butter or margarine,
        softened
    1 cup sugar
    6 egg yolks
    2 cups sifted cake flour
    ½ teaspoon baking powder
    ½ teaspoon salt
    6 egg whites
    ¾ cup sugar
    3 cups whipping cream
    1 tablespoon sugar
    1 teaspoon vanilla
    ½ cup currant jelly
    1 cup coarsely chopped pecans
    1 12-ounce jar strawberry
        preserves (1 cup)

In large mixer bowl, cream together butter or margarine and the 1 cup sugar till very light and fluffy. Add egg yolks, one at a time, beating well after each addition. Beat till very fluffy and smooth, about 5 minutes.

Sift together cake flour, baking powder, and salt; stir into creamed mixture. Beat egg whites until soft peaks form; gradually add the ¾ cup sugar, beating to stiff peaks. Fold egg whites into batter. Pour batter into 3 lightly greased 9x1½-inch round layer cake pans. Bake at 350° for 30 to 35 minutes. Cool.

*To assemble:* Whip cream with the 1 tablespoon sugar and the vanilla. Place one layer of cake on serving plate; spread with currant jelly and *1 cup* of the whipped cream. Sprinkle with *2 tablespoons* of the chopped pecans.

Gently place second layer on cake. Spread top with ⅔ *cup* of the strawberry preserves and *another 1 cup* whipped cream. Sprinkle with *2 tablespoons* chopped pecans.

Gently add third cake layer. Frost top and sides with remaining 1½ cups whipped cream and coat sides with the remaining ¾ cup pecans. Using the tip of a spoon, dot whipped cream-topped cake with remaining ⅓ cup of the strawberry preserves.

### A holiday spectacular

Ruby-red jam made from summer's bright →
berries sparkles atop this Strawberry Torte,
a Christmas tradition from Lithuania.

This melon has been labeled Christmas or Santa Claus because it ripens in storage and can then be enjoyed during the holidays.

**CHRISTMAS MELON**—A large, oblong variety of winter melon (also called Santa Claus melon) identified by its mottled green and gold surface.

Christmas melons usually weigh from six to nine pounds. The flesh is a thick, firm, and juicy yellowish green similar to honeydew melon. A mild and slightly sweet flavor is characteristic in spite of its pungent aroma. (See also *Melon*.)

**CHRISTMAS PUDDING**—Another term for the steamed dessert plum pudding traditionally served in England at Christmas. (See *Christmas, Plum Pudding* for additional information.)

**CHUB**—A small, freshwater fish of the carp family. Several varieties of chubs inhabit the Great Lakes. Soft texture and mild flavor, much like whitefish, make chubs suitable for smoking.

**CHUCK**—The shoulder cut of a beef carcass. Well-known retail cuts of chuck include boneless chuck pot roast, blade pot roast, and arm pot roast, all of which may simply be labeled "chuck roast." Except for the chuck cut called "petite steak," all require slow cooking in some liquid and must be braised. (See also *Beef*.)

## Polynesian Beef Roast

1    3- to 4-pound beef chuck roast
1    large onion, sliced
1    cup pineapple juice
¼    cup soy sauce
1½    teaspoons ground ginger
1    cup diagonally sliced celery
4    carrots, cut in 3- to 4-inch strips
½    pound spinach, cleaned and stems removed *or* 10-ounce package frozen spinach, thawed
2    cups fresh mushrooms, sliced
2    tablespoons cornstarch

In shallow baking dish cover meat with onion. Combine pineapple juice, soy sauce, ginger, and ¼ teaspoon salt. Pour over meat. Marinate 1 hour at room temperature, turning meat once.

Place meat and onions in Dutch oven. Pour pineapple mixture over. Cover; simmer till meat is tender, about 2 to 2½ hours. Add celery and carrots. Sprinkle vegetables with salt; bring to boiling; then simmer 20 minutes.

Arrange spinach and mushrooms atop meat. Simmer till spinach is wilted and other vegetables are crisp-tender, about 10 minutes. Remove meat and vegetables to platter; keep hot. Skim fat from meat juices. Blend together ¼ cup cold water and cornstarch. Stir into juices; cook and stir till thick and bubbly. Serves 6 to 8.

**CHURN**—1. The equipment in which milk or cream is agitated to separate the milk fat in a solid mass from the liquid, thereby making butter. 2. The action by which milk or cream fat is separated. (See also *Butter*.)

**CHUTNEY**—An exotic relish that originated in India and is the principal accompanying condiment for curry and other highly spiced dishes. Chutneys may be puréed or chopped mixtures.

Their pastelike consistency identifies chutneys of India which are usually made fresh daily. The flavors are either sweet (based on ripe fruit) or tart (based on vegetables) and almost always are hot. The commercially bottled Indian chutneys are often based on mangoes and may contain tamarinds, raisins, ginger, and other spices. "Major Grey's" chutney, readily

Baked Chutney Pears play a dual role as meat accompaniment and garnish when served on a platter with roast lamb or ham.

available in the United States, is not a brand name but a specific type of chutney made with green mangoes and marketed by a number of manufacturers.

In American versions of chutney, the fruit is left in rather large pieces with a definite shape. These chutneys are richly spiced, but not always hot, and often hint of the sweet-sour. Traditional homemade relishes called chutneys may include mixtures of ripe or green tomatoes, plums, apricots, pumpkin, apples, or peaches.

Chutneys, puréed or chopped, are delicious accompaniments for cold meats and cheeses, as well as curries. As recipe ingredients or garnishes, chutneys add a distinctive flavor. (See *Curry, Indian Cookery* for additional information.)

## Currant Chutney

Mix ½ cup chutney, cut up; ½ cup red currant jelly, 3 tablespoons dried currants, and 2 tablespoons dry white wine. Serve with curries.

## Baked Chutney Pears

    1 16-ounce can pear halves,
        drained
    1 tablespoon butter or margarine,
        melted
    3 tablespoons chutney

Place drained pears, cut side up, on rack in baking dish. Brush with butter. Spoon about ½ tablespoon chutney in the center of each pear half. Bake at 325° for 15 minutes, or till hot. Serve with ham or lamb. Makes 6 servings.

## Chutney Cheddar Spread

    1 cup shredded natural
        Cheddar cheese
    ¼ cup chopped chutney
    2 tablespoons butter or margarine
    1 teaspoon instant minced onion
    ¼ teaspoon Worcestershire sauce
        Dash bottled hot pepper sauce
        Assorted crackers

Combine first 6 ingredients in small mixer bowl. Beat with electric mixer till fluffy. Serve with assorted crackers. Makes ⅔ cup.

## Orange Chutney Chops

    4 loin pork chops, ¾ inch thick
    ¼ cup water
        • • •
    ½ cup chopped chutney
    ¼ cup sugar
    ¼ cup water
    2 tablespoons lemon juice
    1 medium orange

In heavy skillet brown pork chops well on both sides over medium heat; pour off excess fat. Add the first ¼ cup water; cover and simmer till tender, about 45 minutes. Combine chutney, sugar, the remaining water, and lemon juice. Peel orange and cut in four ½-inch slices. Place over chops. Pour chutney mixture over.

Continue cooking chops, spooning liquid over occasionally, till liquid becomes slightly syrupy, about 10 to 15 minutes. Arrange the chops on a serving platter. Stir pan juices and pour over the chops. Makes 4 servings.

**CIDER**—A fermented and/or sweet beverage made from the juice extracted from apples. France is the largest producer of fermented cider; extensive production is also found in England. Although most kinds of apples can be used, special varieties are required for high-quality cider.

Cider has been commercially important in France for many years. Likewise, English cider is made by highly developed processes in factories, although it was farm oriented until the twentieth century.

In 1908, the French began regulating the labeling of cider: no beverage may be identified as cider unless it is produced entirely from fermented apple juice, or from a mixture of fermented apple and pear juices with or without the addition of water. *Cidre pur juice* is limited to cider made without the addition of water. *Cidre* applies only to a beverage which contains a certain amount of dry extract, ash, and at least 3.5 percent by volume of alcohol. Cider containing a smaller amount of alcohol, extract, and ash is labeled *petite cidre*. English regulations, less strict, forbid the label of cider on any beverage which does not have fermented apple juice as its base.

Since the United States does not produce an alcoholic cider in significant quantity, these European standards do not apply in America. In fact, the use of the term has caused much confusion. American processors label their apple juice products "cider," "apple cider," or "sweet cider;" their choice is determined by the most popular market term. Usually, all three terms refer to pure, unfermented apple juice.

Country cider, produced on local farms and generally sold at roadside stands, may be fermented or partially fermented. Partially fermented cider to which benzoate of soda has been added, may also be labeled as sweet cider, due to its low alcoholic content. Country cider that has been allowed to ferment completely, thus having a much higher alcoholic content, is known as hard cider. Hard cider and imported cider are sometimes available in retail liquor stores.

Hard cider or imported cider are often served alone, much the same as beer is served. Apple cider (unfermented) is popular as a beverage during the fall season. In addition to being used in hot and cold drinks or punches, apple cider lends itself to cooking, for basting and barbecue sauces, and as part of the liquid in gelled salads or baked products. (See also *Apple*.)

## American Hot Mulled Apple Cider

½ cup brown sugar
1 teaspoon whole allspice
1 teaspoon whole cloves
¼ teaspoon salt
　　Dash ground nutmeg
3 inches stick cinnamon
2 quarts apple cider
　　Orange wedges
　　Whole cloves

Combine first 7 ingredients in large saucepan. Bring to boiling. Cover; simmer 20 minutes. Strain to remove spices. Serve in mugs with clove-studded orange wedges. Makes 8 servings.

## Apple Cider Snap

In saucepan combine 1 quart apple cider *or* apple juice and 2 tablespoons red cinnamon candies. Heat and stir till candies dissolve and cider is hot. Serve in mugs with apple-slice floaters. Makes 6 to 8 servings.

**CIDER VINEGAR**—A sour liquid made by controlled fermentation of apple cider, used as a flavoring agent and as a food preservative. Light golden brown, it has a faint taste of apple. Its acidity is due primarily to acetic acid produced during fermentation. Its total acidity usually ranges from four to six percent. Cider vinegar is the vinegar most often preferred in the United States. (See also *Vinegar*.)

### Golden, spicy refreshment

Swirl American Hot Mulled Apple Cider →
with cinnamon stick and add clove-studded orange wedge. Serve in a king-sized mug.

**CINNAMON**—A sweet-pungent spice derived from the dried bark of a tree in the evergreen family. Cinnamon is one of the oldest spices, dating back to 2700 B.C. It has been used for centuries not only to flavor food, but also as a medicine, a perfume ingredient, and an aromatic substance burned as incense. The Greeks made offerings of cinnamon boughs to Apollo; Romans luxuriated in cinnamon-scented baths; and cinnamon-oil candles, rare and costly, were used in medieval churches.

***How cinnamon is produced:*** Although several varieties of cinnamon-producing trees are grown, the processing method is similar for all. At harvest, the dried bark is slit and stripped off both the trunk and branches. It is then rolled into long, slender "quills," known as cinnamon sticks. The quills, sometimes as long as 30 inches, are exported for grinding.

***Types of cinnamon:*** Trees producing cinnamon are in the *Cinnamomum* family. Most of the cinnamon used in the United States is of the *cassia* variety which is coarse, dark, and pungent. The three types of cassia cinnamon on the American market are Saigon cinnamon, Korintje cinnamon, and Padang (Batavia) cinnamon. Saigon cinnamon, imported from South Vietnam, is judged best in flavor because the bark contains a high percentage of essential oil. Korintje and Padang cinnamon are both grown on the island of Sumatra. Korintje rates higher than Padang for its more intense color and flavor.

Ceylon cinnamon, another variety, is much lighter in color, flavor, and aroma than the cassia cinnamons. Although some Ceylon cinnamon is imported here, most of it is reexported to Mexico where it is a popular ingredient in many foods.

***How to store:*** The aroma and flavor of cinnamon are retained much longer in stick form than in ground form. Thus, since ground cinnamon weakens with storage, don't buy it in great quantities—buy small amounts of fresh cinnamon periodically. Cinnamon is best stored in a cool, dry place—excessive heat may weaken the flavor and high humidity causes caking.

***How to use:*** One of the most popular spices, cinnamon is often used in breads, salads, desserts, beverages, and some meat dishes. Ground cinnamon emits flavor more readily than stick cinnamon since grinding cuts through the cell walls, exposing the flavor-bearing oils. Stick cinnamon is most often used for spicing clear liquids that might be clouded by ground cinnamon. Cinnamon sticks also serve as handy, flavorful stirrers for hot beverages. (See also *Spice.*)

## Cinnamon-Raisin Bars

½ cup butter or margarine
1 cup brown sugar
1½ cups sifted all-purpose flour
½ teaspoon baking soda
1½ cups quick-cooking rolled oats
　Raisin Filling
　Cinnamon Icing

Cream butter and sugar. Sift together flour, soda, and ½ teaspoon salt; stir into creamed mixture. Add oats and 1 tablespoon water. Mix till crumbly. Firmly pat *half* the mixture in greased 13x9x2-inch baking dish. Spread with Raisin Filling. Mix remaining crumbs and 1 tablespoon water; spoon over filling. Pat smooth. Bake at 350° for 35 minutes. Cool. Drizzle with Cinnamon Icing. Makes 30.

*Raisin Filling:* In saucepan combine ¼ cup granulated sugar and 1 tablespoon cornstarch. Stir in 1 cup water and 2 cups seedless raisins. Cook and stir till thick and bubbly.

*Cinnamon Icing:* Mix 1 cup sifted confectioners' sugar with ¼ teaspoon ground cinnamon. Stir in enough milk, about 1 tablespoon, for drizzling consistency.

**CINNAMON SUGAR**—A mixture of ground cinnamon and granulated sugar, used as a topping for fruit or to make cinnamon toast. Easily blended at home, it is available on the market in a shaker-top jar.

**CIOPPINO** *(chuh pē' nō)*—A fish stew which supposedly originated in California. Although many variations exist, it is made with both fish and shellfish, tomatoes, onion, wine, and seasonings.

## Cioppino

¼ cup finely chopped onion
3 cloves garlic, minced
1 tablespoon snipped parsley
¼ cup olive oil
1 28-ounce can tomatoes
2 8-ounce cans tomato sauce
½ teaspoon dried oregano leaves,
   crushed
½ teaspoon dried marjoram leaves,
   crushed
½ cup dry sherry
2 12-ounce uncooked rock-lobster
   tails, cut in serving pieces,
   shell and all
1½ pounds whitefish (sole, haddock,
   halibut, *or* cod), cut up
⅔ pound raw cleaned shrimp
   (1 pound in shell)
2 dozen clams in shell* *or* 3
   7½-ounce cans minced
   clams, drained

In Dutch oven cook onion, garlic, and parsley in hot oil till onion is tender. Add tomatoes, next 3 ingredients, 1½ cups water, 1 teaspoon salt, and dash pepper. Cover; bring to boiling. Reduce heat; simmer, uncovered, for 20 minutes. Add sherry; simmer 10 minutes longer.

Stir in remaining ingredients, adding drained clams last. Cover tightly; bring to boiling. Reduce heat; cook slowly for 15 minutes. (Clam shells will pop open during cooking.) Serve in heated soup bowls. Makes 6 servings.

*To prepare clams in shells:* Scrub shells. Allow clams to stand in cold salted water (⅓ cup salt to 1 gallon water) for 15 minutes. Repeat twice. Refrigerate till ready to use.

**CISCO** *(sis' kō)*—A species of whitefish native to the Great Lakes of Canada and the United States. It is sold smoked, then skinned and flaked for use in creamed fish dishes or salads. (See also *Fish.*)

**CITRIC ACID**—An acid which appears naturally in citrus fruits, currants, pineapples, pears, and many berries. It has a pleasant, sour taste. Extracted from lime or lemon juice, it is used commercially as a flavoring agent in a wide variety of foods and carbonated beverages.

**CITRON**—A citrus fruit grown chiefly for its thick peel which is candied and used as a baking ingredient, especially in fruitcakes. It resembles a lemon but is longer and yellow green in color. Citron is grown primarily in Mediterranean countries and the West Indies.

Depending upon the variety of citron, the pulp may be acid or sweet. In either case, the pulp is used only for by-products; the peel from either type is the main product. The peel is first soaked in brine or seawater to remove the bitter oil and to intensify the flavor. It is then candied in sugar before marketing.

Candied citron is available halved or diced in various sized jars or sold in bulk. It should be moist and slightly sticky; if hard and crystallized, it has been stored too long. (See also *Citrus Fruit.*)

## Fruit Bread

2 cups sifted all-purpose flour
¾ cup sugar
3 teaspoons baking powder
½ teaspoon salt
2 beaten eggs
1 cup milk
3 tablespoons salad oil
¼ cup diced candied citron
¼ cup dried currants
2 tablespoons finely diced
   candied cherries
2 tablespoons diced candied
   lemon peel
½ cup chopped walnuts

Sift together first 4 ingredients. Combine eggs, milk, and salad oil; add to flour mixture, beating well (about ½ minute). Stir in fruits and nuts. Turn into greased 9x5x3-inch loaf pan. Bake at 350° about 50 minutes. Remove from pan; cool on rack. Wrap and store overnight.

**CITRON MELON**—A member of the watermelon family, it is inedible raw. Much harder than the popular watermelon, it has a white flesh and red seeds. Sometimes known as preserving melon, the flesh of the melon is candied with sugar and used in making conserves.

# CITRUS FRUIT

*How to add tangy flavor and vivid color to
any meal with these vitamin-rich fruits.*

Tart and fresh-flavored fruits of citrus trees comprise a large group known as citrus fruit, the most familiar being the orange, lemon, lime, grapefruit, kumquat, citron, tangerine, mandarin, and tangelo.

These fruits have a long, intriguing history. They originated in the tropical regions of Asia and from there were taken into the Mediterranean area. In the twelfth century, Crusaders returning from the Holy Lands introduced many varieties of citrus fruits to their European countries.

Citrus fruits became popular because of their nutritive value as well as their taste appeal. These fruits, especially rich in vitamin C (ascorbic acid), were found to prevent the disease scurvy. The British Navy provided their sailors with limes during long voyages to prevent the disease. This is the origin of the nickname "limey" for British seamen. These seamen were particularly fond of the limes when the juice was mixed with gin.

Citrus fruits were brought to America by Columbus. On his second voyage, from 1493 to 1496, citrus trees were planted in Haiti. More were planted in the area around St. Augustine, Florida, in 1565.

During the California Gold Rush, many prospectors developed scurvy because of a lack of fresh fruit. Lemons, very much in demand, sold for as much as one dollar each. Commercial planting of citrus trees in California began at this time, marking the advent of California's citrus industry.

## Exotic citrus fruit

← Eat the tangelo in segments or use its juice and peel for heavenly Tangelo Chiffon Pie. Tangerine can be substituted in the pie.

The use of citrus fruits has grown steadily in America. In fact, consumption has more than tripled since 1900. The average American eats 80 to 90 pounds of citrus fruit products each year—oranges account for about two-thirds of this total.

***How citrus fruits are grown:*** Citrus trees grow well in tropical and subtropical regions. There are three major areas in the United States where the fruit is grown commercially: the southeast area including Florida and the Gulf States, the western including California and Arizona, and the Rio Grande Valley area of Texas.

Fruit from these areas differs in some aspects. The western area, with its bright sunshine and low humidity, produces brightly colored fruit and juice. The southeastern fruit has somewhat more juice. Fruit produced in the Texas valley has a blend of characteristics of both the western and southeastern fruit.

To produce citrus fruit, trees are usually grown by budding or grafting onto a seedling from a parent tree rather than grown from seeds. Within five or six years these trees will bear a crop.

Citrus trees can have blossoms, immature fruit, and ripe fruit all at the same time. When this occurs, the ripe fruit may be tinged with green color because the tree produces green chlorophyll for the new blooms. This "regreening" does not affect the quality. Once ripened, unlike most fruits, citrus fruit can remain on the tree for weeks or months without becoming overripe or losing quality.

The harvesting, packing, and processing of citrus fruits are highly organized and mechanized. If some ripe fruits show a green color when harvested, they are treated to make their color typical.

Ethylene gas treatment restores the color of fruit grown in the western area. Fruit from the southeastern area gets a coloring bath that brings out the color in the skin. These treatments make the fruit acceptable to consumers but do not affect the flavor or edibility of the fruit pulp or peel.

Juices are extracted mechanically for canning, then blended for optimum quality and flavor, pasteurized, and canned under vacuum. Frozen concentrated juices are made by a moisture-evaporation process which eliminates the water and are then frozen in tubes for packaging.

With improved production and shipping facilities, United States producers meet the rapidly increasing demand for citrus fruit in American markets, plus exporting fruit to many foreign countries.

*Nutritional value:* Citrus fruits are excellent sources of vitamin C. One or two servings of citrus fruit will supply the daily recommended amounts of vitamin C for adults and children.

Depending on the type and variety, citrus fruits also contain varying amounts of vitamin A, the B vitamins, and minerals. Fresh citrus fruits have a low calorie count, usually less than 60, which makes them doubly attractive to dieters.

*How to select:* A selection of top-quality citrus fruits is available throughout the year in the markets. Choose those fruits which are firm, a characteristic color, shiny, and free from blemishes. Heavier fruits contain more juice.

Sizing can be a guideline for the consumer when purchasing citrus fruit. Sizes are assigned according to the number of fruit packed into a standard-size box. For instance, a carton of oranges sized as 56's contains 56 oranges. The larger the number per box, the smaller the fruit. Therefore, lemons sized as 95's are larger than those sized as 115's.

The quality, flavor, and amount of juice in the fruit per box will be the same regardless of the size of the fruit. Selection of which size to buy should be made according to the size that is most plentiful at that time, the size you prefer, and how you plan to use the fruit.

*How to store:* Citrus fruits can be kept in the covered fruit or vegetable section of the refrigerator for several weeks. Wrap the fruit in perforated, clear plastic bags if it is to be stored in another part of the refrigerator. If the peel has been grated, always cover the fruit in foil or clear plastic wrap to keep it from drying out.

Most citrus fruits can be frozen for extended storage. The juice or sections are prepared for freezing by sweetening with sugar and adding ascorbic acid color keeper to preserve the best quality. Use these frozen fruits within 8 to 12 months.

# Types of citrus fruit

Citrus fruits come in an array of bright colors and tart flavors. Each type has its own special characteristics and uses.

*Citron:* This yellow green fruit resembles a lemon. However, citrons are larger than lemons, measuring about six to nine inches in length and have thicker rinds.

Citron is grown for its rind rather than its acid pulp. It is the rind that appears on the market as candied and preserved citron and in packages of mixed candied fruit for use in fruitcakes and cookies.

*Grapefruit:* Grapefruits vary in color from pale yellow to russet to bronze. The tart-sweet pulp may be seedy or seedless. The Marsh, Duncan, and Ruby are the common varieties on the market.

Grapefruit halves, eaten chilled or broiled, can perk you up at breakfast or whet your appetite at dinner. The sections and juices are used as ingredients in recipes. The shaddock, a probable ancestor of grapefruit, often grows as large as a watermelon and weighs 15 to 20 pounds.

*Kumquat:* The smallest member of the citrus family, it has a sweet rind and an acid pulp. Orange in color and oblong to round in shape, kumquats are used in preserves and Oriental dishes.

*Lemon:* Yellow, oval, and very sour lemons are used to enhance many foods. They add flavor and tartness to salads, fish, beverages, sauces, vegetables, and desserts.

Arranged in basket are lemons, limes, and Navel oranges. Around basket (right to left) are tangelos, tangerines, Marsh seedless and Ruby Red grapefruits, and Valencia oranges.

*Lime:* The lime, very acid in flavor, has a green, smooth peel. It is about the same size and shape as the lemon. Limes and lemons are used in the same ways and sometimes may be used interchangeably.

*Limequats* are a tart, pale yellow hybrid developed from lime and kumquat.

*Mandarin:* Small and deep orange, mandarins are round in shape but slightly flattened at the ends. Mandarins are loose-skinned so the rind can be removed easily.

*Tangerines, satsumas,* and *temple oranges* are actually varieties of mandarin. The *calamondin* is a mandarinlike citrus fruit from the Philippines.

*Orange:* The most popular of the citrus fruits has a color ranging from light orange to deep red. Navel and Valencia are the best-known varieties. Navels are seedless and have a small "navel" formation at the blossom end. Valencias are practically seedless and especially juicy.

Oranges are excellent to eat out-of-hand and to use in countless dishes.

*Tangelo:* This hybrid was developed in 1897 by crossing the tangerine and grapefruit. This juicy fruit has a sweet but tart flavor. The rind resembles that of an orange but the flesh is a pale yellow. A tangelo may be used like a tangerine.

*Ugli:* Well named, ugli fruit is an unattractive, puffy fruit—in appearance, but not in flavor. It tastes like orange, grapefruit, and tangerine all in one. Limited numbers are imported from Jamaica.

*Forms available:* Citrus fruits and citrus fruit products can be purchased in many forms to meet a variety of purposes.

Whole fruit and sections are available fresh, canned, and frozen. These may be packaged separately by types or mixed with other fruits. Juices are also available fresh, canned or bottled, and frozen—as one flavor or a blend of several flavors, concentrated or natural strength.

Other forms of citrus fruit include candied peel, extract, citrus-flavored gelatins and powdered mixes, and liqueurs, such as curacao and Cointreau.

# Uses of citrus fruit

Citrus fruit can be used in any course of a meal and enjoyed at any time of the day. Some appetizers, beverages, salads, entrées, breads, desserts, and snacks are made with one or more citrus fruits as the major ingredient or flavor accent.

As an appetizer, citrus fruits are especially good because their tartness stimulates the appetite without satisfying it.

## Frosted Cocktail

*Pass a tray of hors d'oeuvres with these non-alcoholic cocktails—*

> ½ cup sugar
> ⅔ cup lemon juice
>
> • • •
>
> ⅔ cup pineapple juice
> 2 tablespoons lime juice
> 2 unbeaten egg whites
> 4 cups finely crushed ice

Cook sugar and ⅔ cup water for 5 minutes; chill. Add lemon juice, pineapple juice, lime juice, egg whites, and crushed ice. Pour *half* the mixture into blender container. Blend till light and frothy, 7 or 8 seconds. Repeat with second half. Serve at once in chilled cocktail glasses with short straws. Serves 8 to 10.

## Spiced Citrus Appetizer Cup

> 1 16-ounce can mixed grapefruit
>    and orange sections,
>    undrained (2 cups)
> 3 inches stick cinnamon
> Dash ground cloves
> Dash ground ginger
> Maraschino cherries

Combine all ingredients in saucepan; simmer for 10 minutes. Remove cinnamon stick. Chill. Serve in small glass dishes. Garnish with maraschino cherries. Makes 4 or 5 servings.

Beverages are frequently made using citrus juice as a base or accented with just a dash of juice. Punches and ades owe their refreshing, not-too-sweet flavor to the citrus base. Mixed drinks, such as the daiquiri, Margarita, and screwdriver, are also made with a citrus foundation.

## Citrus Cooler

> ¼ cup frozen orange-grapefruit
>    juice concentrate, thawed
> 1 pint lemon sherbet
> 1 12-ounce bottle ginger ale

Pour thawed concentrate into electric blender container. Add ¾ cup icy cold water and sherbet. Cover; blend 15 seconds. Divide mixture among 4 chilled glasses. Slowly pour in chilled ginger ale to fill each glass. Stir gently; serve *immediately.* Makes 4 servings.

## Tangy Citrus Fizz

> ¾ cup cold orange juice
> 1 cup vanilla ice cream
> ½ cup lemon sherbet
> 1 teaspoon aromatic bitters
> 1 7-ounce bottle lemon-lime
>    carbonated beverage

In electric mixer bowl or blender containers, combine juice, ice cream, sherbet, and bitters. Beat or blend till smooth. Pour into 2 tall glasses. Carefully pour in carbonated beverage. Stir gently. Makes 2 servings.

Citrus fruit sections or slices along with crisp lettuce are often used in salads, in molded mixtures, or on fruit platters. Tangy salad dressings also are made with the addition of citrus fruit juice.

## Spiced Mandarin Mold

    1 11-ounce can mandarin orange
        sections
    ¼ teaspoon salt
    6 inches stick cinnamon
    ½ teaspoon whole cloves
            • • •
    2 3-ounce packages orange-flavored
        gelatin
    3 tablespoons lemon juice
    ½ cup broken walnuts

Drain mandarins; reserving syrup. Add water to syrup to make 1¾ cups. In saucepan, combine syrup mixture, salt, cinnamon, and cloves. Cover and simmer 10 minutes; remove from heat. Let stand covered 10 minutes. Strain.

Add gelatin to syrup mixture; stir over low heat till gelatin is dissolved. Add 2 cups cold water and lemon juice. Chill till partially set. Stir in mandarins and nuts; turn into a 6½-cup mold. Chill till firm. Serves 6 to 8.

## Low-Cal Fruit Bowl

    1 medium grapefruit, chilled
    2 medium oranges, chilled
    1 ripe medium banana
    1 cup chilled sliced fresh
        strawberries
    ½ cup chilled honeydew balls
        Lettuce
        Mint sprigs
        Low-Cal Snow Dressing

Peel and section grapefruit and oranges, reserving juices. Peel and slice banana; brush with reserved fruit juices. Combine grapefruit and orange sections, banana, strawberries, and honeydew balls in lettuce-lined bowl. Garnish with mint. Serve salad with Low-Cal Snow Dressing. Makes 4 servings.

*Low-Cal Snow Dressing:* Combine 1 cup plain yogurt, 4 teaspoons sugar, 1 teaspoon lemon juice, and dash salt. Chill thoroughly.

## Heavenly Orange Fluff

    2 3-ounce packages orange-
        flavored gelatin
    1 13½-ounce can crushed pineapple
    1 6-ounce can frozen orange juice
        concentrate, thawed
    2 11-ounce cans mandarin oranges,
        drained
    1 3¾-ounce package *instant*
        lemon pudding mix
    1 cup cold milk
    1 cup whipping cream

Dissolve gelatin in 2½ cups boiling water; add undrained pineapple and concentrate. Chill till partially set. Fold in mandarins; pour into 13x9x2-inch pan. Chill till firm. Beat pudding and milk with rotary beater till smooth. Whip cream and fold into pudding. Spread over gelatin; chill. Makes 12 to 15 servings.

To section citrus fruit: first peel and remove excess membrane. Then cut into center between one section and membrane. Slide knife down other side of section next to membrane.

## Orange-Apricot Ring

    2 16-ounce cans apricot halves
    2 3-ounce packages orange-flavored
        gelatin
    1 6-ounce can frozen orange juice
        concentrate
    2 tablespoons lemon juice
    1 7-ounce bottle (about 1 cup)
        lemon-lime carbonated
        beverage, chilled

Drain apricots, reserving 1½ cups syrup. Purée apricots in sieve or blender. Heat reserved apricot syrup to boiling; dissolve orange-flavored gelatin and dash salt in syrup. Add purée, juice concentrate, and lemon juice; stir till concentrate is melted. Slowly pour chilled carbonated beverage down side of pan; mix gently. Pour gelatin mixture into 6½-cup ring mold. Chill till firm. Makes 10 to 12 servings.

## Summer Fruit Platter

*Add this salad to the buffet menu—*

    Whole fresh pineapple
    Apples
    Fresh pears
    Fresh strawberries, sliced
            • • •
    Oranges, sliced crosswise
    Cantaloupe wedges
    Stewed prunes, drained
    Lime Honey *or* Marshmallow
        Blizzard

Chill fruit. Halve pineapple lengthwise; remove hard core. Scoop out fruit and cut into chunks. Cube apples and pears; toss with pineapple chunks and sliced strawberries. Pile fruit mixture into pineapple shells. Arrange on a tray with orange slices, cantaloupe wedges, and prunes. If desired, garnish with sprigs of mint. Serve Lime Honey *or* Marshmallow Blizzard Dressing with the fruit platter.

*Lime Honey:* Blend together ¼ cup honey with 2 tablespoons lime juice. Add dash salt.

*Marshmallow Blizzard:* To half of 7-ounce jar marshmallow creme, add 1 tablespoon *each* orange juice and lemon juice. With electric or rotary beater, beat till very fluffy. Fold in ¼ cup mayonnaise or salad dressing.

## Fluffy Citrus Dressing

    1 egg
    ½ cup sugar
    1 tablespoon grated orange peel
    2 teaspoons grated lemon peel
    2 tablespoons lemon juice
    1 cup whipping cream

In saucepan beat egg; add sugar, peel, and lemon juice. Cook and stir over *low* heat till thick, 5 minutes. Cool well. Whip cream and fold into egg mixture. Chill. Makes 2⅓ cups.

Citrus fruits make attractive garnishes or accompaniments with entrées, as well as adding flavor to the meat dishes, to sauces for meat, and to stuffings.

## Orange Pot Roast

    1½ teaspoons salt
    ½ teaspoon ground cumin
    ¼ teaspoon ground cloves
    ⅛ teaspoon pepper
    1 3- or 4-pound chuck pot roast
    1 tablespoon shortening
    1 6-ounce can frozen orange juice
        concentrate, thawed
            • • •
    1 cup bias-cut celery slices
    1 5-ounce can bamboo shoots,
        drained
    1 11-ounce can mandarin oranges,
        drained
    1 tablespoon cornstarch

Combine salt, cumin, cloves, and pepper. Make small slits in chuck roast; in each slit insert some of the spice mixture. Melt shortening in large skillet or Dutch oven. Brown meat on both sides. Add concentrate and ¾ cup water. Cover and simmer till tender, 2½ to 3 hours.

Add celery; simmer, covered, 10 to 12 minutes. Arrange bamboo shoots and mandarin oranges on top of roast. Cook, covered, 5 to 7 minutes. Remove meat to warm platter.

Skim fat from liquid. Blend cornstarch and 2 tablespoons cold water; slowly add to liquid in pan, stirring constantly. Cook and stir till thick. Serve gravy with meat and pass vegetables in serving bowl. Makes 6 to 8 servings.

## Mediterranean Sauce

¼ cup brown sugar
1 tablespoon cornstarch
⅛ teaspoon salt
⅛ teaspoon ground cloves
1 cup orange juice
2 tablespoons lemon juice
½ cup chopped dried figs

In saucepan combine brown sugar and cornstarch. Blend in salt, cloves, orange juice, and lemon juice. Bring to boil, stirring constantly. Add figs; cover and simmer 5 minutes. Serve sauce hot with pork. Makes 1½ cups sauce.

Vegetable flavors are often sparked by zesty citrus juice. The juice can be added to vegetables or to the sauces for the vegetable. Citrus peel or segments also add a colorful appearance and distinctive taste.

## Ambrosia Potato Bake

½ lemon, thinly sliced
½ orange, thinly sliced
6 to 7 cups sliced, cooked *or* canned sweet potatoes, drained

• • •

1 8¾-ounce can crushed pineapple
½ cup brown sugar
½ cup butter, melted
½ teaspoon salt

• • •

½ cup shredded coconut
Maraschino cherries

Alternate lemon, orange, and sweet potato slices in an 11½x7½x1½-inch baking dish. Combine crushed pineapple, brown sugar, butter, and salt; pour over potatoes and fruit. Sprinkle coconut over top; garnish with cherries. Bake at 350° for 30 minutes. Serves 8 to 10.

### A showcase dessert

Delicately flavored with orange and lemon, Citrus Chiffon Pie is a treasured recipe to make for those extra special occasions.

Breads can be flavored with citrus peel or juice in the dough, filling, or glaze. A hint of citrus in the fragrance of freshly baked bread gives it a tantalizing aroma.

## Citrus Coffee Cake

    2 tablespoons butter or margarine
    1 tablespoon frozen orange juice
        concentrate, thawed
    1 teaspoon lemon juice
    ⅓ cup sugar
    ¼ teaspoon ground cinnamon
    ¼ cup coarsely chopped pecans
    1 8-ounce package refrigerated
        buttermilk biscuits

Melt butter in 8x1½-inch round cake pan. Stir in orange juice concentrate, lemon juice, sugar, cinnamon, and chopped pecans. Top with biscuits. Bake at 350° for 25 minutes. Cool 1 minute; invert on serving plate. Serve warm.

## Orange Coffee Braid

    2 packages active dry yeast
    5 to 5½ cups sifted all-purpose
        flour
 1¼ cups milk
          • • •
    ½ cup sugar
    ⅓ cup frozen orange juice
        concentrate, thawed
    6 tablespoons butter or margarine
    1 teaspoon shredded lemon peel
    ½ teaspoon salt
    1 egg
          • • •
    ¾ cup sifted confectioners' sugar
    1 tablespoon frozen orange juice
        concentrate, thawed
        Toasted slivered almonds

In large mixer bowl, combine yeast and 2⅔ *cups* flour. Heat milk, sugar, ⅓ cup juice, butter, peel, and salt just till warm, stirring occasionally to melt butter. Add to dry mixture in mixing bowl; add egg. Beat at low speed with electric mixer for ½ minute, scraping sides of bowl constantly. Beat 3 minutes at high speed. By hand, stir in enough of remaining all-purpose flour to make a soft dough.

Turn out on lightly floured surface and knead till smooth, about 8 to 10 minutes. Place in greased bowl, turning once to grease surface. Cover and let rise in a warm place till doubled, about 1½ hours. Punch down; divide dough in half and let rest about 10 minutes.

From one-half of dough, cut off one-third and set aside. Divide remaining two-thirds into three equal portions. Roll each portion into a 12-inch strand. Place the three strands on greased baking sheet and braid.

Divide reserved one-third of dough into three equal portions and roll each portion into 12-inch strand. Braid and place atop first braid. Repeat with second half of dough, forming two braids as before. Cover; let rise till almost doubled, about 45 minutes. Bake at 350° for 30 to 35 minutes.

Beat together the confectioners' sugar, 1 tablespoon thawed orange juice concentrate, and 1 tablespoon water. Brush over tops of braids when they come from the oven. Sprinkle tops with almonds. Makes 2 braids.

Desserts made with citrus fruit are colorful and flavorful. The citrus flavor can be incorporated into cake, pastry, pie, pudding, sauce, and ice cream. Citrus segments, twists, cartwheels, curls, and shredded peel are attractive as garnishes on desserts. (See *Fruit* and individual citrus fruits for additional information.)

## Orange Velvet

    1 3-ounce package orange-
        flavored gelatin
    ½ cup sugar
    1 cup water
    1 cup light corn syrup
    1 cup orange juice
    2 tablespoons lemon juice
    2 cups milk
    2 cups light cream

In saucepan combine gelatin and sugar; stir in water and corn syrup. Bring to boiling, stirring till gelatin dissolves. Remove from heat. Stir in juices; cool. Add milk, cream, and a dash salt. Freeze in ice cream freezer according to freezer directions. Garnish servings with orange slices, as desired. Makes 2 quarts.

## Citrus Cobbler

1 16-ounce can grapefruit sections
1 11-ounce can mandarin orange
  sections
½ cup brown sugar
3 tablespoons all-purpose flour
7 tablespoons butter or margarine
1 cup sifted all-purpose flour
1 tablespoon granulated sugar
1½ teaspoons baking powder
1 slightly beaten egg

Combine *undrained* fruits; divide among 6 individual bakers or place in 8x8x2-inch baking dish. Mix brown sugar with the 3 tablespoons flour; sprinkle over fruit. Dot with *3 tablespoons* butter or margarine. Heat at 425° for 15 minutes. Sift together 1 cup flour, granulated sugar, baking powder, and ¼ teaspoon salt; cut in the remaining butter. Add enough milk to egg to make ½ cup; stir into dry ingredients. Drop mixture by spoonfuls on hot fruit to form biscuits. Sprinkle with a little sugar and cinnamon. Bake at 425° for 20 to 25 minutes or till biscuits are lightly browned. Serve warm with cream, if desired. Makes 6 servings.

## Mandarin Soufflé

¼ cup sugar
1 envelope unflavored gelatin
4 well-beaten egg yolks
¾ cup tangerine *or* orange juice
2 tablespoons lemon juice
2 tablespoons grated orange peel
4 egg whites
2 tablespoons sugar
1 cup whipping cream

In a saucepan combine the ¼ cup sugar and gelatin; blend in egg yolks, then tangerine or orange juice, and lemon juice. Cook and stir over low heat till gelatin dissolves and mixture thickens slightly. Stir in orange peel; cool mixture to room temperature.

Beat egg whites to soft peaks; gradually add 2 tablespoons sugar, beating to stiff peaks. Whip cream. Fold gelatin into egg whites, then fold in whipped cream. Turn into a 5-cup melon mold. Chill overnight or till set. Unmold on platter. Garnish with whipped cream and mandarin oranges, if desired. Serves 6 to 8.

## Tangelo Chiffon Pie

1 envelope unflavored gelatin
½ cup sugar
4 eggs, separated
½ cup lemon juice
¾ cup tangelo *or* tangerine juice
½ teaspoon grated lemon peel
½ teaspoon grated tangelo *or*
  tangarine peel
⅓ cup sugar
1 9-inch *baked* pastry shell*

In a saucepan mix gelatin, ½ cup sugar, and dash salt. Beat together egg yolks and fruit juices; stir into gelatin. Cook and stir over medium heat till mixture comes to boiling. Remove from heat; mix in peels. Chill, stirring occasionally, till partially set. Beat egg whites till soft peaks form. Gradually add ⅓ cup sugar; beat to stiff peaks. Fold in gelatin. Pile into pastry shell; chill till firm. Garnish with dollops of whipped cream and tangelo *or* tangerine sections, if desired.

## Citrus Chiffon Pie

1 envelope unflavored gelatin
½ cup sugar
4 egg yolks
½ cup orange juice
⅓ cup lemon juice
½ teaspoon grated orange peel
½ teaspoon grated lemon peel
4 egg whites
⅓ cup sugar
1 9-inch *baked* pastry shell*

In saucepan thoroughly mix gelatin, the ½ cup sugar, and dash salt. Beat together egg yolks, juices, and ¼ cup water; stir into gelatin. Cook and stir over medium heat just till mixture comes to boiling and gelatin is completely dissolved. Remove from heat; stir in orange and lemon peel. Chill, stirring occasionally, till mixture is partially set.

Beat egg whites till soft peaks form. Gradually add the ⅓ cup sugar, beating till stiff peaks form; fold in gelatin mixture. Pile into cooled baked pastry shell. Chill till firm. Garnish with whipped cream and a sprinkle of shredded orange peel, if desired.

*(See *Pastry* for recipe.)

**CITY CHICKEN**—Boneless cubes of veal threaded together on a skewer and then cooked. The skewered cubes are coated with crumbs, browned, and then baked in a small amount of liquid. (See also *Veal*.)

## City Chicken

      2 pounds veal, cut in 1½-inch
        cubes
      ⅔ cup fine saltine cracker crumbs
   1½ teaspoons salt
      1 teaspoon paprika
      ¾ teaspoon poultry seasoning
      1 slightly beaten egg
      2 tablespoons milk
      3 tablespoons shortening
      1 chicken bouillon cube

Thread veal cubes onto 6 short skewers. Combine crumbs, salt, paprika, and poultry seasoning. Combine egg and milk. Dip meat in egg mixture, then in crumbs. Brown slowly on all sides in hot shortening. Dissolve bouillon cube in ½ cup boiling water; add to meat. Cover; bake at 350° for 45 minutes. Uncover; bake 30 minutes more. Makes 6 servings.

**CIVET** *(siv' it)*—A French stew made with rabbit or other furred game, wine, onion, mushrooms, and seasonings. The blood of the animal is used to thicken the stew.

**CLABBER**—Unpasteurized milk that has soured naturally and formed a thickened mass in which there is no separation of curd from whey. Sometimes called bonny-clabber, it is popular in some countries served chilled as a beverage. When thickly clotted, it is eaten as a dessert; sugar and flavoring may be added. (See also *Milk*.)

**CLAM**—A shellfish in which the edible flesh is encased in two shells joined together at the back. Prized for their distinctive flavor, clams are a part of many traditions. Undoubtedly, the most elaborate and ceremonial is the "clambake." First staged by the Indians, it involves cooking clams, fish, and corn on heated stones in a shallow pit. Covered with wet rockweed, the food is cooked by steam. Today's clambakes often include additional foods such as lobster and chicken, but the cooking method is the same. For an inland clambake, substitute a barbecue grill for the open pit and a wet canvas for the wet rockweed.

## Individual Clambake

   48 soft-shelled clams, in shells
      8 live whole lobsters
      4 2- to 2½-pound ready-to-cook
        broiler-fryer chickens, halved
      ½ cup butter or margarine, melted
      8 whole ears of corn
        Rockweed
      1 pound butter, melted

Thoroughly wash clams in shells. Cover with salt water (⅓ cup salt to 1 gallon water); let stand 15 minutes. Rinse; repeat twice. Rinse off lobsters with salt water. For chickens, break joints of drumstick, hip, and wing so birds will stay flat. Brush chickens with ½ cup melted butter or margarine; broil over *hot* coals, skin side down for about 5 minutes.

Turn back husks of corn and strip off silk with a stiff brush. Lay husks back in position.

Tear off 3-foot lengths of 18-inch wide heavy foil. Place 1 sheet crosswise over another sheet. Repeat making total of 8 individual packages. Lay a handful of rockweed in center of each. Cut eight 18-inch squares cheesecloth; place 1 square atop rockweed in each package.

For each package arrange the following: 6 live clams in shells, 1 live lobster, 1 precooked chicken half, and 1 ear of corn. Securely tie cheesecloth around meat and vegetable, opposite ends together. Seal the foil, opposite ends together, using the drugstore wrap. Place on grill, seam side up, over *hot* coals and cook for 45 minutes. To test for doneness, the chicken drumstick should move up and down easily in socket. When the chicken is done, the clambake is ready. Serve with individual cups of hot melted butter. Makes 8 servings.

### *Modern clambake*

Rockweed adds authenticity to Individual →
Clambake cooked on a grill. Watermelon and cold beer complete the outdoor feast.

***How clams are harvested:*** Clam digging is not only an amateur's delight but also a commercial business. Clamming on a small scale involves digging with your hands or a rake-type instrument for the **soft clams** found in the tidal flats. Commercially, fishermen employ long-handled rakes, tongs, or dredges for digging hard clams living at much greater depth.

***Nutritional value:*** Clams provide protein and minerals including phosphorus, calcium, and iron. Relatively low in calories, four large soft-shell clams or five hard clams contain about 80 calories.

***Types of clams:*** Several varieties of clams are marketed, each supplied from a different coastal region. The hard clam (round clam), the soft-shell clam (longneck clam), and the surf clam are found along the Atlantic coast. The hard clam is given the Indian name *quahog* in the New England area where the term clam is used only for the soft-shell variety. In the Middle Atlantic states and southward, clam refers to the hard clam.

The soft-shell clam, found in the tidal flats, appears chiefly in the Chesapeake Bay although some are found farther north. The hard clam, often living more than 50 feet deep, is found south of Cape Cod down to Texas. Surf clams live along the Middle Atlantic coastline.

The small-sized hard clams are divided into littlenecks and cherrystones and are served raw on the half shell. The larger hard clams, called chowder clams, are used for chowders and soups. Soft-shell clams are also divided into classes: the larger sizes are known as in-shells, and the smaller sizes are called steamers.

The Pacific coast varieties of clams include Pismo, razor, geoduck, Washington or butter, heart cockle, and rock cockle (rock clam or common littleneck). Each varies in flavor and use but should not be confused with the Atlantic varieties.

***How to select:*** Clams are available in the shell, shucked, or canned. When purchasing hard clams, gently tap each shell. It should close tightly to indicate the clam is alive. A gaping shell that does not close means that the clam is dead and should not be used. With other varieties, a constriction of the siphon (tube through which clam takes in food and oxygen and eliminates wastes) is noticeable when touched. Clams in the shell are sold by the dozen or by the pound.

If the clam muscle has been removed from the shell, the clams are sold as shucked clams. Packaged in various-sized containers, they should appear plump with clear liquor and be free of shell particles. Shucked clams are also available frozen.

Many varieties of clams are preserved by canning and are marketed either whole or minced. Other clam products available include chowder, juice, broth, and nectar.

***How to store:*** Shell clams will remain alive and fresh for several days if refrigerated immediately after being dug or purchased. Shucked clams, too, require refrigeration and may be stored for several days when properly handled. Frozen clams should not be thawed until ready to use and after thawing, they should not be refrozen.

***How to prepare:*** Wash clams thoroughly to remove all surface sand. Allow clams to stand in cold salt water (⅓ cup salt to 1 gallon water) for 15 minutes. Rinse and repeat two more times. This permits clams to open and discharge sand which then settles to the bottom of container.

Clams may be shucked either before or after cooking, depending upon how they are served. To open clams, insert knife between shell halves and pry apart (see page 564). If steamed before shucking, the shell will open during steaming. The shells of soft clams and surf clams are not as tight-fitting and so are easier to open.

***How to use:*** Clams served on the half shell make an elegant appetizer. Discard the top shell, cut the muscle free but leave it in the bottom half shell. Other clam appetizers include dips and canapés.

The popular clam chowder, with its many regional variations, is often considered a specialty. Clams are also used in seafood salads, casseroles, soufflés, or other main dishes. Fried clams are also favorites. (See also *Shellfish.*)

## Clam Puff

- 2 7½-ounce cans minced clams
  Milk
- 1 cup fine saltine cracker crumbs
  (24 crackers)
- 2 tablespoons instant minced onion
- 4 well-beaten eggs
- 2 tablespoons snipped parsley
- ½ teaspoon salt
  Dash bottled hot pepper sauce

Drain clams, reserving liquor; add milk to liquor to make 1 cup. Combine milk mixture with crumbs and minced onion. Let stand 15 minutes. Fold in clams, eggs, parsley, salt, and bottled hot pepper sauce. Pour into *ungreased* 1½-quart soufflé dish. Bake at 325° till knife inserted off center comes out clean, about 60 to 65 minutes. Makes 6 servings.

## Clam Cocktail Dunk

- 2 3-ounce packages cream cheese,
  softened
- 2 teaspoons lemon juice
- 3 drops onion juice
- 1 teaspoon Worcestershire sauce
- ¼ teaspoon salt
- 3 drops bottled hot pepper sauce
- 1 7½-ounce can minced clams,
  chilled and drained
- 1 tablespoon snipped parsley

In small mixing bowl combine softened cream cheese, lemon juice, onion juice, Worcestershire sauce, salt, and bottled hot pepper sauce. With electric or rotary beater, beat till light and fluffy. Stir in drained clams and snipped parsley. Serve clam dunk with assorted crackers or crisp relishes. Makes 1¼ cups.

A delicacy for dining—Steamed Clams served in a big mesh steamer. Accompany with clam broth, melted butter, and lemon wedges. For ease-of-eating, provide guests with bibs.

To open hard-shell clam, hold shell in palm of hand with hinge against palm. Insert slender knife between shell halves.

Carefully cut around clam between shell halves, twisting knife slightly to pry open shell. Lift up top shell-half with thumb.

Cut clam muscle free from each shell half. To serve clam on the half shell, remove one-half of shell before serving.

## Steamed Clams

> 2 dozen soft-shell clams in shells (steamers)
> Salt
>
> • • •
>
> Butter or margarine, melted
> Lemon wedges

Thoroughly wash clams. Cover with salt water, using ⅓ cup salt to 1 gallon cold water. Let stand 15 minutes; rinse thoroughly. Repeat soaking in salt water two more times.

Place clams in shells on rack in kettle. Add 1 cup hot water; cover tightly and steam just till shells open, about 5 minutes. Drain off broth and reserve. Serve in shell or cut out and serve on the half shell (see directions at left). Serve clams with reserved clam broth, melted butter, and lemon wedges. Makes 4 servings.

## Clam-Mushroom Bake

> 1 dozen large hard-shell clams (½ cup clam meat) *or* 1 7½-ounce can minced clams, drained
> 1 3-ounce can chopped mushrooms, drained
> ¼ cup chopped onion
> 3 tablespoons butter or margarine
>
> • • •
>
> 2 tablespoons all-purpose flour
> Dash salt
> Dash pepper
> ½ cup milk
>
> • • •
>
> ½ cup soft bread crumbs
> 2 tablespoons butter or margarine, melted

For fresh clams, prepare Steamed Clams (see above) *or* open unsteamed clams (see directions at left). Remove edible portion; chop.

Cook mushrooms and onion in 3 tablespoons butter till tender but not brown. Blend in flour, salt, and pepper. Add milk all at once. Cook quickly, stirring constantly, till mixture is thickened and bubbly. Stir in clams. Pour into 4 baking shells. Combine bread crumbs and melted butter; sprinkle atop each shell. Bake at 400° till lightly browned, about 10 to 15 minutes. Makes 4 servings.

**CLAM CHOWDER**—A thickened soup made with clams and usually containing salt pork or bacon, potatoes, and/or other vegetables. Popular where its ingredients are readily available, clam chowder is the subject of a continuous controversy about its "true" character. Although many variations exist, most of the debate concerns the liquid used. New England-style clam chowder is made with milk; Manhattan-style clam chowder uses water and tomatoes or tomato juice. (See also *Chowder.*)

## Hogate's Clam Chowder

    2 dozen medium hard-shell clams
    2 ounces salt pork (¾ cup), diced
    2 cups diced, peeled potatoes
        (about 3 medium)
    1 cup chopped onion
    1 teaspoon dried thyme leaves,
        crushed
    1 16-ounce can tomatoes
    2 tablespoons all-purpose flour

Thoroughly wash clams. Cover with salt water (⅓ cup salt to 1 gallon cold water). Let stand 15 minutes. Rinse; repeat 2 more times. Place clams on rack in kettle; add 6 cups hot water. Cover tightly; steam just till shells open, 5 to 10 minutes. Remove clams reserving 4 cups cooking liquor. Shuck clams and dice.

Brown salt pork in large saucepan. Add *2 cups* of the reserved liquor, potatoes, onion, and thyme. Cook till potatoes are almost tender, about 20 minutes. Add tomatoes and remaining 2 cups reserved liquor. Bring to boiling.

Blend all-purpose flour with ¼ cup cold water. Stir into chowder; cook, stirring constantly, till thickened and bubbly. Add diced clams; heat through. Makes 8 servings.

**CLARET** *(klar' it)*—A light, red table wine. All red wines from Bordeaux are commonly termed claret by the British and Americans. However, the clarets of today are not the same as those wines which were originally labeled claret. During the early history of wine making, red wines were fermented only briefly, sometimes for only two weeks—the time it took to ship the wine from France to England.

Many of the classic Bordeaux wines are named after the wine estate or château where they are produced. The first growth of finest wines are Château Margaux, Château Lafite, Château Latour, and Château Haut-Brion. Other less expensive but good clarets are labeled for the Bordeaux district from which they come: Médoc, St. Émilion, Graves, and Pomerol.

The production of fine clarets, however, is not limited to European vineyards. California claret is one of the most popular, domestic red wines on the market. Made from the Cabernet Sauvignon grape, it is labeled Cabernet or Cabernet Sauvignon.

Although personal preference determines the selection and use of red dinner wines, claret is generally served with meat. Used as an ingredient in cooking, it adds a distinctive flavor to many well-known meat dishes. It is a favorite used in preparing the rich sauces which are often served with game, such as pheasant and quail. (See also *Wines and Spirits.*)

## Beef Claret Barbecue

    ½ cup salad oil
    ½ cup claret
    2 tablespoons finely snipped
        candied ginger
    2 tablespoons catsup
    2 tablespoons molasses
    ½ teaspoon salt
    ½ teaspoon curry powder
    ½ teaspoon pepper
    1 large clove garlic, minced
                • • •
    1 pound sirloin steak, cut in
        1-inch cubes
                • • •
    1 green pepper, cut in
        1-inch squares

In glass bowl or shallow dish, combine all ingredients except meat and green pepper. Add beef cubes; let stand at room temperature for 1 hour, or refrigerate overnight. Remove beef cubes, reserving marinade. Arrange on skewers with green pepper squares. Cook over *medium-hot* coals for 12 to 15 minutes, brushing several times with marinade. (Use rotating skewer or turn once during cooking.) Serves 3 or 4.

**CLARIFIED BUTTER**—Clear, oil-like butter poured from melted butter leaving water and salt behind. As butter melts over low heat or hot water, without stirring, the fat rises and the brine sinks to the bottom. When cooled, the oil-like top layer can be carefully poured off.

Clarified butter is called for in a number of French sauce recipes because it can be heated to high temperatures without burning or browning. It is also particularly suitable for quickly sautéing delicately flavored foods. (See also *Butter*.)

**CLARIFY**—To make a liquid or fat clear by separating solid particles from the liquid. One example is the melting of butter to clarify it. To clarify hydrogenated fat that has been used for deep-fat frying, pour an equal amount of hot water over the fat; heat for 10 minutes. Strain through a cloth. Chill until the layer of clarified fat is hard, then drain off the water.

**CLARY**—An herb, one of the strong-scented mints, whose leaves and flowers are used for flavoring foods and beverages. Clary, which tastes like a mixture of mint and sage, is easily grown in herb gardens. It was formerly used like sage in cooking, but now its main use is as one of the herbs used to flavor vermouth. (See also *Herb*.)

**CLEAVER**—A heavy, hatchetlike, wide-bladed utensil with a squared, blunt end. A meat cleaver is used to chop through bony tissue in meats or poultry, and its broad side is used to flatten certain meat cuts as when butterflying chops or tenderloin slices. (See also *Utensil*.)

**CLOTTED CREAM**—Very thick, rich cream that has coagulated after being scalded. (See also *Devonshire Cream*.)

**CLOVE** *(segment)*—A segment of a large plant bulb, such as garlic.

**CLOVE** *(spice)*—Nail-shaped, reddish brown, dried bud used as a spice. This fragrant spice grows on a 30- to 40-foot tropical evergreen tree. The name clove comes from the word for nail, *clou* in French or *clavus* in Latin.

Little is known about the history of cloves, but records of the third century B.C. in China report the use of cloves as a breath sweetener, as when courtiers were ordered to hold cloves in their mouths when addressing the emperor.

Large clove forests were first discovered on the Molucca or Spice Islands in the Indian Ocean. Early explorers were impressed by the beauty of the clove tree and the spicy fragrance wafting from the trees. These explorers noted that natives of these islands planted a clove tree at the birth of each child and prized them as a record of ages: a tribe's strength could be noted by the number of trees it had.

During the Middle Ages, all spices reaching Europe had to be carried overland, for the most part, by way of Egypt. This slow means of import made cloves an extremely expensive item—a pound (4,000 to 7,000 cloves) of this spice cost $20.

Between the fourteenth and seventeenth centuries, the major European powers raced each other to find the closest sea routes to the Spice Islands. The establishment of these water routes led to wars between Europeans and native islanders to secure rights to the clove business. Although the islanders fought fiercely, they were greatly outnumbered and soon lost the spice trade to the Europeans.

During the seventeenth century, the Dutch gained control of the Spice Islands and thus controlled the majority of clove trees. To ensure complete control, the Dutch destroyed all clove trees growing on other islands, confining production to their own territory. In 1760, when spice prices failed to satisfy the Dutch, they attempted to raise prices by burning large numbers of cloves and nutmegs at Amsterdam.

The Dutch spice monopoly was maintained for over a century. It was broken in 1770 when the Governor of Mauritius, an island near Madagascar, stole clove seeds and started growing them on his island.

Ironically, although the finest cloves are still found on the Spice Islands, these are not exported but are used by the Indonesians to scent tobacco. Today, the world's supply of this spice comes mainly from the islands of Madagascar and Zanzibar, off the east coast of Africa.

The unopened clove buds must be hand picked at exactly the right stage of maturity to be useful as a spice. Harvest season lasts from October to February.

After being picked, the cloves are spread on mats where they are dried by exposure to the sun and smoke from wood fires. During this six to eight day period, cloves turn from red to a deep brown color and lose at least half of their original weight.

Cloves imported into the United States arrive in whole form. Grinding companies thoroughly clean all the cloves and then grind a portion of them. Both whole and ground cloves are available on the grocery store spice shelf.

The strong, pungent-sweet flavor of cloves seems to "belong" to ham. A small piece of clove flavor perks up condiments, fruit butters, relishes, pickled fruits, spiced cakes and cookies, mincemeat, chocolate dishes, pork roast, stewed fruits, and apple pie. An onion studded with a few cloves adds a subtle spicy flavor to stew. A little of this strong, aromatic spice adds a lot of flavor, so remember to use cloves sparingly. (See also *Spice*.)

## Refrigerator Crisps

    1 cup shortening
    ½ cup granulated sugar
    ½ cup brown sugar
    1 egg
    2 tablespoons milk
    2¼ cups sifted all-purpose flour
    ½ teaspoon baking soda
    ½ teaspoon salt
    1 teaspoon ground cinnamon
    ¼ teaspoon ground nutmeg
    ¼ teaspoon ground cloves
    ½ cup finely chopped walnuts

Cream together shortening and sugar. Add egg and milk; beat well. Sift together flour, baking soda, salt, cinnamon, nutmeg, and cloves; stir into creamed mixture. Stir in finely chopped walnuts. Shape in rolls 2½ inches in diameter. Wrap in waxed paper; chill well.

Slice about ¼ inch thick. Place 1 inch apart on lightly greased cookie sheet. Bake at 375° till delicately browned, about 5 to 7 minutes. Remove at once to rack. Makes 6 dozen.

## Spicy Apricot Mold

    1 16-ounce can apricot halves
    1 8¾-ounce can pineapple tidbits
    2 tablespoons vinegar
    1 teaspoon whole cloves
    4 inches stick cinnamon
        • • •
    2 3-ounce packages orange-
        flavored gelatin
    ¾ cup boiling water
    ¾ cup apricot nectar
    ½ cup dairy sour cream

Drain the apricot halves and pineapple tidbits, reserving syrups. Combine syrups with vinegar, whole cloves, and stick cinnamon; bring to boil. Simmer 10 minutes; strain. Add hot water to make 2 cups. Pour over *one* package orange-flavored gelatin; stir to dissolve gelatin. Chill till mixture is partially set.

Fold in *well-drained* apricot halves, halved, and pineapple. Pour into 6½-cup ring mold. Chill till mixture is *almost* firm.

Meanwhile, dissolve remaining package orange-flavored gelatin in boiling water; stir in apricot nectar. Chill till mixture is partially set; whip till fluffy. Swirl in dairy sour cream. Pour sour cream mixture over first layer. Chill till firm, at least 8 hours. Makes 8 servings.

## Pickled Onion Rings

*Pile these on hamburgers for a special flavor —*

    1 cup water
    1 cup white vinegar
    ¼ cup sugar
    ½ teaspoon salt
    6 inches stick cinnamon,
        broken in pieces
    2 teaspoons whole cloves
    10 drops red food coloring
    1 large sweet onion, thinly
        sliced and separated in
        rings (about 4 cups)

In small saucepan combine water, white vinegar, sugar, salt, stick cinnamon, and whole cloves. Simmer, covered, 10 minutes; strain. Add food coloring; pour hot mixture over onion rings. Chill at least 4 hours, turning occasionally. Drain thoroughly before serving.

Club cheese—
A soft, spreadable
cheese blend.

**CLUB CHEESE**—A cheese product made by blending one or more aged, sharp, natural cheeses. Although club cheeses originated in Canada, they are extensively produced in the United States today. Natural cheeses are ground and mixed without heating or pasteurizing and then packed cold—thus, the name cold-pack often given to club cheese. Condiments, wine, or flavorings such as smoke are often added to the cheese. The resulting club cheese is soft, spreadable, and keeps well when stored in the refrigerator.

Usually packaged in jars, rolls, or links, club cheeses make flavorful additions to appetizers, snacks, sandwiches, and desserts. (See also *Cheese*.)

## Cheese-Stuffed Mushrooms

    2  6-ounce cans broiled mushroom
        crowns*, drained (2 cups)
    1  tablespoon finely chopped onion
    1  teaspoon salad oil
              •   •   •
    ¼  cup finely chopped salami
    ¼  cup smoke-flavored cheese
        spread (club cheese)
    1  tablespoon catsup
        Fine soft bread crumbs

Hollow out mushroom crowns and chop enough pieces to make 3 tablespoons; in skillet cook mushroom pieces and onion in oil. Stir in salami, cheese spread, and catsup. Stuff into mushroom crowns; sprinkle with crumbs. Bake on baking sheet at 425° till hot, about 6 to 8 minutes.

*Or use 2 pints fresh mushrooms. Wash; trim off tips of stems. Remove stems and chop enough to make ⅓ cup. Continue as above.

**CLUB SANDWICH**—A hearty triple-decker sandwich made with three toast slices. The filling layers consist of various meats—usually chicken, turkey, bacon, or ham—lettuce, and tomato. (See also *Sandwich*.)

## Club Sandwich

    3  slices toasted sandwich bread
        Butter or margarine
              •   •   •
        Lettuce
        Sliced cooked chicken *or*
            turkey
        Mayonnaise or salad dressing
    2 or 3 thin slices tomato
    2 or 3 slices cooked bacon

Spread toast with butter. Top first slice with lettuce and chicken *or* turkey. Spread with mayonnaise or salad dressing. Top with second toast slice. Add tomato and bacon. Top with third toast slice. Anchor with 4 wooden picks. Cut diagonally in quarters. Makes 1 serving.

**CLUB STEAK**—The first steak cut from the center loin section of beef, usually identified by a rib bone along its side. The large muscle is the loin eye. (See *Beef, Steak* for additional information.)

**COAGULATE**—To change the form of a food from a liquid or semiliquid to a solid or semisolid substance. Examples of coagulation include the formation of a tender milk curd when rennet is added to slightly warm milk, or the solidification of semiliquid egg white and semisolid egg yolk when egg is heated.

**COAT**—To cover one food with a layer of another, such as flour, bread crumbs, or sugar, in order to add texture to the food or to protect its inner moistness.

Coating may involve one of two techniques. A food may itself be moist enough to coat with a fine substance as when cookies hot from the oven are rolled in sugar. When the outer surface of a food is dry, or a thicker coating is desired, the food is first dipped in a liquid, often water, beaten egg, butter, or milk, then in the coating.

The quick and neat method to coat chicken —shake the chicken pieces with the dry crumb mixture in a plastic bag.

By dipping the chicken pieces first in flour, second in egg-water mixture, and third in crumbs, a crisper cooked coating is achieved.

Another coating method involves rolling the chicken pieces in melted butter, then in the desired crumb mixture.

**COBBLER**—1. The name for a beverage made of wine or liquor, fruit or fruit juice, and sugar. 2. A deep-dish baked fruit dessert of American origin made with top crust only. The crust is usually made with biscuit dough rather than pastry; however, this point may be argued in some parts of the country where the pastry topping is preferred. (See also *Dessert*.)

## Fruit Cobblers

*A basic biscuit topper with fruit variations—*

> 1 cup sifted all-purpose flour
> 2 tablespoons sugar
> 1½ teaspoons baking powder
> ¼ teaspoon salt
> ¼ cup butter or margarine
> ¼ cup milk
> 1 slightly beaten egg
> Apple, Cherry, Peach, *or* Rhubarb Filling
> Light cream *or* ice cream

For biscuit topper sift together flour, sugar, baking powder, and salt. Cut in butter or margarine till mixture resembles coarse crumbs. Combine milk and slightly beaten egg. Add all at once to dry ingredients, stirring just to moisten. Set mixture aside.

Prepare Apple, Cherry, Peach, *or* Rhubarb filling. Pour hot filling into 8¼x1¾-inch round ovenware cake dish. Immediately spoon on biscuit topper in 6 mounds. Bake at 400° for 20 to 25 minutes. Serve warm with light cream or ice cream. Makes 6 servings.

## Apple Filling

*For a treat, serve with cinnamon ice cream—*

> 1 cup sugar
> 2 tablespoons all-purpose flour
> ½ teaspoon ground cinnamon
> ¼ teaspoon ground nutmeg
> 6 cups sliced peeled apples

Combine sugar, flour, cinnamon, and nutmeg in saucepan. Toss apples with sugar mixture. Cook and stir over medium heat till apples are *almost* tender, about 7 minutes.

Crunchy pecans and tangy orange peel give the golden biscuits in Spring Rhubarb Cobbler a new dimension. Serve this dessert any season using fresh or frozen rhubarb as available.

## Cherry Filling

1 20-ounce can pitted tart red cherries (water pack), undrained
½ cup sugar
1 tablespoon quick-cooking tapioca
Few drops red food coloring

· · ·

1 tablespoon butter or margarine

Combine cherries, sugar, tapioca, and food coloring in saucepan. Let stand 5 minutes. Cook and stir till slightly thickened and bubbly, about 5 minutes. Stir in butter.

## Peach Filling

½ cup brown sugar
½ cup water
1½ tablespoons cornstarch
¼ teaspoon ground mace

· · ·

4 cups sliced peaches
1 tablespoon lemon juice
1 tablespoon butter or margarine

Combine brown sugar, water, cornstarch, and ground mace in saucepan. Cook, stirring constantly, till mixture is thickened and bubbly. Add peaches, lemon juice, and butter. Cook till peaches are hot, about 5 minutes.

## Rhubarb Filling

    1 cup sugar
    2 tablespoons cornstarch
 1/4 teaspoon ground cinnamon

          •   •   •

    4 cups 1-inch pieces fresh rhubarb
    1 tablespoon water
    1 tablespoon butter or margarine

Combine sugar, cornstarch, and cinnamon in saucepan. Add rhubarb, water, and butter. Bring to boiling. Cook and stir 1 minute.

## Spring Rhubarb Cobbler

 1/3 cup sugar
     Dash ground cinnamon
 1½ cups ½-inch pieces fresh rhubarb*
 ½ cup water
     Few drops red food coloring

          •   •   •

    2 teaspoons butter or margarine
      Biscuit Topper

In small saucepan combine sugar and cinnamon. Add rhubarb, water, and food coloring. Cook and stir till mixture boils; cook 2 minutes more. Stir in butter or margarine. Pour rhubarb sauce into 2-cup baking dish or 2 individual casseroles. Spoon Biscuit Topper over *bubbling hot* sauce. Bake at 400° for 25 to 30 minutes. Serve with cream, if desired. Serves 2.

*Biscuit Topper:* Sift together ⅓ cup sifted all-purpose flour, 2 tablespoons sugar, ½ teaspoon baking powder, and dash salt. Cut in 1½ tablespoons butter. Stir in 2 tablespoons milk, 2 tablespoons chopped pecans, and ¼ teaspoon shredded orange peel. Push from spoon into two dollops atop *bubbling hot* fruit.

*\*For frozen rhubarb:* Thaw and drain half of a 16-ounce package frozen rhubarb, reserving syrup. Add enough water (about ⅔ cup) to syrup to make 1 cup. Blend 2 tablespoons sugar, 2 teaspoons cornstarch, and dash ground cinnamon in small saucepan; stir in rhubarb syrup and few drops red food coloring. Cook and stir till mixture bubbles. Add drained rhubarb and 2 teaspoons butter; heat through. Pour into 2-cup baking dish or 2 individual casseroles. Spoon Biscuit Topper (above) over *bubbling hot* sauce. Bake at 400° for 25 to 30 minutes. Serve with light cream, if desired. Serves 2.

## Peach–A–Berry Cobbler

 1/4 cup brown sugar
    1 tablespoon cornstarch
 ½ cup cold water
    2 cups sugared sliced fresh
        peaches*
    1 cup fresh blueberries*
    1 tablespoon butter or margarine
    1 tablespoon lemon juice

          •   •   •

    1 cup sifted all-purpose flour
 ½ cup granulated sugar
 1½ teaspoons baking powder
 ½ teaspoon salt
 ½ cup milk
 1/4 cup butter or margarine,
        softened
    2 tablespoons granulated sugar
 1/4 teaspoon ground nutmeg

In saucepan mix brown sugar and cornstarch; add water. Stir in peaches and berries. Cook and stir till mixture thickens (about 3 minutes after mixture boils). Add the 1 tablespoon butter or margarine and lemon juice. Pour into 8¼x1¾-inch round ovenware cake dish.

Sift together flour, the ½ cup sugar, baking powder, and salt. Add milk and softened butter all at once; beat smooth. Pour over hot fruit. Mix the 2 tablespoons sugar and nutmeg. Sprinkle over batter. Bake at 350° till done, about 40 to 45 minutes. Serve warm with light cream, if desired. Makes 6 servings.

*Or use canned or frozen fruits. Drain; use ½ cup syrup instead of water.

## Orange Cherry Cobbler

    1 21-ounce can cherry pie filling
 1/4 cup water
    1 tablespoon lemon juice
    1 package refrigerated orange
        Danish rolls with icing
        (8 rolls)

In saucepan combine pie filling, water, and lemon juice; heat to boiling. Pour into 8¼x1¾-inch round ovenware cake dish. Top *hot* cherries with rolls, cut side up. Bake at 400° until rolls are done, about 15 to 20 minutes. Spread tops with the icing that comes in the orange-roll package. Serve warm. Makes 8 servings.

**COCK-A-LEEKIE**—A Scottish soup made with chicken broth, cut-up pieces of cooked chicken, and leeks. Sometimes prunes and raisins are added; however, the modern version contains no fruit.

**COCKLE**—A saltwater mollusk with fluted, heart-shaped shells that is harvested on seacoasts throughout the world where the cockle finds sand beds in which to live. With the shell ranging in size from about ½- to 9-inches in diameter and having a brown, yellow, or red color, they are usually sold in the United States, shelled, cooked, and canned. You'll find cockles on the gourmet shelf in grocery stores and in specialty food shops. Cockles are sweet-tasting and can be eaten raw, cooked like clams and oysters, or used in making delicious soups. (See also *Shellfish*.)

**COCKTAIL**—An alcoholic or nonalcoholic beverage, or fruit or seafood appetizer normally served before the meal.

Alcoholic cocktail beverages are mixed, iced drinks, served in glasses of all sizes. Cocktails are based on a distilled spirit, such as gin, whiskey, vodka, or rum. The exact origin of these alcoholic drinks is not known, although they are said to have originated in America during the time of Revolutionary War.

A cocktail party is a good way to entertain when space is limited. Since most of the guests remain standing, little seating space is required. Although cocktails are the main item served, appetizers and hors d'oeuvres also are offered for guests to nibble as they sip their cocktails. (If the cocktail party precedes a dinner, keep the appetizers and cocktails light.)

One of the most popular cocktails is the dry martini, a mixture of gin or vodka and dry vermouth. It can be mixed ahead of time, then chilled until serving time. Other cocktails include the Manhattan, old-fashioned, bacardi, daiquiri, or whiskey sour. If only one kind of cocktail is offered at the cocktail party, offer bourbon and/or scotch, and some nonalcoholic beverage for the abstainers.

Prepare cocktails in a shaker with ice, filling the shaker only half to two-thirds full so that the contents can be thoroughly shaken. The shaker should be large enough for a round of drinks. Two or more shakers may be used if there are a large number of guests. Cracked ice is used to chill the liquids quickly and to help mix the drink. Then, use a cocktail strainer to keep the ice in the shaker while pouring the cocktail into individual glasses.

If a shaker is not handy, cocktails can be mixed with a long-handled spoon in a pitcher. Some say that a stirred cocktail is not as diluted as a shaken cocktail.

The cocktail is often served in a glass with a stem or, if the drink is served "on the rocks" (with ice), in a short glass. It should be pleasing to the eye. That's why some cocktails are garnished with fruit or colored with fruit juices.

Nonalcoholic cocktails include fruit cups made of thoroughly chilled and attractively arranged fruit, cut in small pieces. They can be served in sherbet glasses, glass bowls, icers, or in a variety of attractive glasses. These cocktails, too, should be pleasing to the eye and may be trimmed with such colorful items as maraschino cherries or fresh mint leaves. If the fruit cocktail is the first course of a meal, do not make the servings too large.

Seafood cocktails may also be served as appetizers and may include shrimp, crab, or lobster cocktails topped off with a zippy sauce. Keep the portions small—this course is designed to stimulate the appetite, not dull it.

Nonalcoholic beverage cocktails most generally have a fruit or vegetable juice as the base. However, in recent years, undiluted canned beef bouillon, served on the rocks, has become an accepted first-course cocktail. (See *Beverages, Wines and Spirits* for additional information.)

## Summer Fruit Cocktail

In a bowl mix 2 cups sliced, peeled peaches; 1 cup diced, peeled pears; and ½ to 1 cup fresh blueberries. Combine ¼ cup lemon juice, ½ cup sugar, and dash salt, stirring to dissolve the sugar. Pour over fruits in bowl. Toss. Chill thoroughly. Spoon into stemmed sherbet glasses and garnish each serving with a fresh mint sprig. Makes 5 or 6 servings.

## 1-2-3 Fruit Cup

    1 13½-ounce can pineapple
        tidbits (1⅔ cups)
    1 10-ounce package frozen
        raspberries, thawed
    3 tablespoons orange-flavored
        breakfast drink powder
    1 11-ounce can mandarin oranges,
        drained

Drain pineapple tidbits and thawed raspberries, reserving syrups. Stir together reserved syrups and breakfast drink powder. Divide pineapple, raspberries, and oranges among 6 sherbet glasses; pour on syrup mixture. Serves 6.

## Pineapple Cocktail

    2 cups unsweetened pineapple
        juice
    1 cup apple juice
    2 tablespoons lemon juice
    1 pint pineapple sherbet
        Fresh mint

Combine pineapple, apple, and lemon juices; pour into juice glasses and chill. Just before serving, top each glass with a small scoop of pineapple sherbet and a sprig of fresh mint. Makes 6 to 8 servings.

## Tomato Zip

*A good dinner beginner—*

    2¾ cups tomato juice
    ⅔ cup condensed beef broth
    ¼ cup water
    1 teaspoon Worcestershire sauce
    ½ teaspoon onion juice
    ½ teaspoon prepared horseradish
        Dash pepper
    3 or 4 lemon slices

In saucepan combine tomato juice, beef broth, water, Worcestershire sauce, onion juice, prepared horseradish, and pepper. Add lemon slices and heat just to boiling; remove and discard lemon slices. Serve hot. If desired, garnish each serving with an additional fresh lemon slice. Makes 4 to 6 servings.

## Shrimp Cocktail

        Cleaned, cooked shrimp
    ¾ cup chili sauce
    2 to 4 tablespoons lemon juice
    1 to 2 tablespoons prepared
        horseradish
    2 teaspoons Worcestershire sauce
    ½ teaspoon grated onion
        Dash bottled hot pepper sauce
        Lettuce

Chill shrimp. Meanwhile, combine chili sauce, lemon juice, prepared horseradish, Worcestershire sauce, onion, and bottled hot pepper sauce. Add salt to taste. Chill thoroughly.

Line chilled cocktail cups with lettuce. Add 4 or 5 chilled shrimp to each cocktail cup. Spoon cocktail sauce over shrimp. Serve with cocktail forks. Makes 1¼ cups sauce.

**COCOA**—1. A powdery food product made from cacao beans. It contains less cocoa butter than does chocolate. 2. A beverage made from the powdery substance with the addition of either milk or water.

The processing of cocoa is the same as that used for chocolate up to the point where the nibs are made into the chocolate liquor. This liquid is processed through a hydraulic press to squeeze out part of the fat, called cocoa butter. The hard mass or cakes that remain are then crushed, ground, and sifted until they become the fine cocoa powder that is sold.

Cocoa adds some fat to the diet in addition to minerals. One cup of cocoa beverage made with milk has 235 calories.

How much fat cocoa adds to the diet depends on its type. Breakfast or high-fat cocoa contains at least 22 percent cocoa butter and is the type available to most consumers. Medium-fat cocoa contains 10 to 22 percent cocoa butter; whereas, low-fat cocoa contains less than 10 percent fat. These last two types are purchased predominantly for commercial use by bakers and confectioners. None of these types of cocoa have added sugar.

There are other types of cocoa available in grocery stores. One is called Dutch-type or Dutch-process cocoa. To make this type of cocoa, an alkaline salt is added to the

Try a new use for cocoa. Make Cocoa Ripple Ring for breakfast, brunch, or afternoon treat. Either unsweetened cocoa or presweetened instant cocoa powder mix can be used.

cacao beans or chocolate liquor. This partially neutralizes the natural acids present in the cacao bean. As a result, the beverage prepared with Dutch-process cocoa will be darker in color, will have a different flavor and finer aroma, and will not settle out in the cup as readily.

Ready-to-use or instant cocoa powder mixes are also available. These mixes contain sugar, flavorings, and sometimes dried milk, in addition to the cocoa powder. Depending on the type of cocoa that is used, simply add water or milk—hot or cold— and enjoy a delightful beverage.

Store all types of cocoa in a cool, dry place in a tightly covered container to prevent the mixture from lumping.

Cocoa powder has many uses, not only as a beverage, but in baking and cooking. In baking, cocoa powder is usually blended with the dry ingredients. In a beverage, it is best to cook the cocoa with sugar and a small amount of water before adding the milk. This eliminates the raw, starchiness of the cocoa and keeps cocoa solids from settling to the bottom of the cup as quickly. Instant cocoa powder can also be used to make a delicious cake topper.

Cocoa can be substituted in a recipe calling for unsweetened chocolate if shortening is added. The substitution is 3 tablespoons unsweetened cocoa powder plus 1 tablespoon fat equals 1 ounce unsweetened chocolate. (See also *Chocolate*.)

# Breakfast Cocoa

In a saucepan mix ⅓ cup unsweetened cocoa powder, ⅓ cup sugar, and dash salt; add ½ cup water. Bring to boiling, stirring constantly. Boil 1 minute. Stir in 3½ cups milk. Heat just to boiling point but *do not boil*. Add ½ teaspoon vanilla; beat with rotary beater just before serving. Float dollops of marshmallow creme atop each serving. Makes 4 cups.

# Cocoa Ripple Ring

Cream together ½ cup shortening, ¾ cup sugar, and 2 eggs till light and fluffy. Sift together 1½ cups sifted all-purpose flour, 2 teaspoons baking powder, and ¾ teaspoon salt. Add to creamed mixture alternately with ⅔ cup milk, beating well after each addition. Spoon a *third* of the batter into a well-greased 6½-cup mold or 9x9x2-inch baking pan.

Combine ⅓ cup instant cocoa powder mix* and ⅓ cup chopped walnuts. Sprinkle *half* of the cocoa mixture over batter in pan. Repeat layers, ending with batter. Bake at 350° for 35 minutes. Let stand 5 minutes. Turn out of mold. Serve warm. Makes 12 servings.

*Or, substitute ¼ cup sugar and 2 tablespoons unsweetened cocoa powder for the mix.

# Cocoa Fudge Cake

   ¾ cup butter or margarine
1½ cups sugar
   3 eggs
1½ teaspoons vanilla
   1 teaspoon red food coloring
2¼ cups sifted cake flour
   ½ cup unsweetened cocoa powder
   3 teaspoons baking powder

Cream butter and sugar till light. Separate eggs. Add yolks, one at a time, beating well after each. Add vanilla and food coloring. Sift together dry ingredients. Add to creamed mixture alternately with 1 cup cold water, beating after each addition.

Beat egg whites till soft peaks form. Fold into batter. Bake in 2 greased and floured 9x 1½-inch round cake pans at 350° till done, about 25 minutes. Cool 10 minutes before removing from pans. Cool completely; frost.

# Chocolate Daisy Cupcakes

   ½ cup butter or margarine
1½ cups sugar
   2 eggs
   2 cups sifted all-purpose flour
   ¼ cup unsweetened cocoa powder
   1 teaspoon baking soda
   ½ teaspoon salt
      •   •   •
   2 teaspoons instant tea powder
   1 cup cold water
   1 teaspoon vanilla
   1 can ready-to-spread chocolate
      frosting
   Whole blanched almonds

Cream butter and sugar together till light and fluffy. Add eggs, one at a time, beating well after each. Sift together flour, cocoa powder, baking soda, and salt.

Dissolve tea in the cold water; add vanilla. Alternately add dry ingredients and tea mixture to creamed mixture, beating well after each addition. Line muffin pans with paper bake cups. Fill each half-full. Bake at 350° about 20 minutes. Cool completely. Frost with the chocolate frosting. Arrange whole nuts on each to make a "daisy." Makes 2 dozen cupcakes.

Cocoa powders include Dutch-process cocoa (left), unsweetened cocoa (center), and instant ready-to-use cocoa mix (right).

teaspoon salt. Add to creamed mixture, blending well. Shape in rolls about 2 inches in diameter. Wrap in waxed paper; chill 4 to 6 hours.

Slice rolls into thin cookies and place on *ungreased* cookie sheet. Bake at 350° for 6 to 8 minutes. Makes about 6 dozen cookies.

## Minted Cocoa Fluff

Combine 1 cup whipping cream, ½ cup instant cocoa powder mix, and 1 or 2 drops peppermint extract; chill. Whip till stiff.

Serve on slices of angel food cake; top each serving with crushed peppermint stick candy. Makes 1½ cups topping.

## Peanut Butter-Oatmeal Bars

    ½ cup shortening
    ½ cup granulated sugar
    ½ cup brown sugar
    ⅓ cup peanut butter
    ½ teaspoon vanilla
    1 egg
    ¼ cup milk
        • • •
    1 cup sifted all-purpose flour
    ½ teaspoon baking soda
    1 cup quick-cooking rolled oats
    2 cups sifted confectioners'
        sugar
    ¼ cup unsweetened cocoa powder
    3 tablespoons butter, melted
    ½ teaspoon vanilla
        Icing

Cream together first 5 ingredients till fluffy. Add egg and milk; beat well. Sift together flour, baking soda, and ½ teaspoon salt. Add to creamed mixture. Beat just till combined. Stir in rolled oats. Spread mixture evenly in greased 13x9x2-inch baking pan. Bake at 350° for 20 minutes. Cool thoroughly.

Sift together confectioners' sugar and cocoa. Quickly stir in melted butter, 2 to 3 tablespoons boiling water, and ½ teaspoon vanilla. Beat till smooth. Spread quickly and evenly over cooled cookies in pan.

*Icing:* Heat and stir 2 tablespoons butter or margarine till golden brown. Stir in 1 cup sifted confectioners' sugar and 3 to 4 teaspoons milk. Drizzle over cookies. Cut in bars.

Dress-up wedges of fluffy angel cake with easy Minted Cocoa Fluff. Pass crushed peppermint candy for a colorful topper.

## Cocoa-Mint Wafers

    1 tablespoon vinegar
    ¼ cup milk
    ½ cup shortening
    1 cup sugar
    1 egg
    ¼ to ½ teaspoon peppermint
        extract
    2 cups sifted all-purpose flour
    ½ cup unsweetened cocoa powder
    ½ teaspoon baking soda

Add vinegar to milk; set aside. Cream together shortening and sugar. Add egg, extract, and milk. Sift together remaining ingredients and ¼

COCONUT, COCOANUT—The fruit of the coconut palm. It is used as a beverage, as a food, and as a cooking oil.

Often found growing along the sandy seashore, the wide distribution of the coconut palm is due to the sturdy character of its fruit. The coconut, relatively light in weight, has a fibrous husk with a leathery skin that prevents it from becoming waterlogged. When dropped from trees growing along the shore into the sea, the coconuts are carried by tides and currents to distant shores where they germinate readily on sandy beaches. Today, coconut palms are found abundantly in Indonesia and other southeast Asian countries, the Philippines, and tropical America.

The coconut palm matures in about seven years and will produce fruit for 70 to 80 years. When unripe or green, the coconut is filled with a rich, cold milk. This is an important beverage on the tropical islands. The milk is always cold because of the insulation provided by the meat of the fruit. After the milk and meat are removed, the shell of the coconut is often used as a water cup on the islands.

In addition to producing coconuts, the tree is a source of numerous other products, some of which have significant commercial value. The young buds are cut out of the top of the tree and cooked as a vegetable, known as "palm cabbage"; the tree sap is used in making wine, liquor, and vinegar; the trunk provides lumber; the leaves are used for making fans, baskets, and thatched roofs; and the husk of the coconut yields a durable fiber, important in making ropes, cords, and brushes.

Copra (dried coconut meat), the major export product of many of the smaller islands, is pressed to obtain coconut oil. A white, solid substance at room temperature, it is used for cooking and for manufacturing candles, soap, and margarine. Coconut oil is also used in making suntan lotions and other toiletry items.

*Nutritional value:* One-fourth cup of fresh, shredded coconut provides about 84 calories while dried, shredded coconut has a somewhat higher caloric value. In addition, coconut contains very small amounts of some vitamins and minerals.

*How to select:* Fresh coconuts are available throughout the year in most markets, but the peak season is from October through December. Select those that are heavy for their size and whose liquid can be heard sloshing around inside when shaken. Avoid coconuts without milk and those whose three soft spots or "eyes" at the top of the shell are wet and moldy.

Coconut is also available in the supermarket shredded, grated, or flaked. Marketed in various sized cans or packages, it may be dry or moist, sweetened or unsweetened. It is also available toasted.

*How to store:* An uncracked coconut may be stored at room temperature for one to two months. Once it is cracked, it should be refrigerated in a tightly covered container. Freshly grated coconut can be kept three to four days in the refrigerator or stored for many months in the freezer.

Packaged coconut stays fresh on the kitchen shelf in the unopened container for several months. After opening, it must be refrigerated in a tightly covered container to maintain freshness. Like freshly grated coconut, the storage life of packaged coconut is prolonged if frozen.

*How to prepare:* The husk and shell of the coconut must be removed before the meat can be eaten or prepared for use in baking. First, using a sharp instrument such as an ice pick, pierce the three eyes of the coconut and drain the milk. Then tap all over with a hammer until the shell cracks and falls off or can be pulled off.

Another method for removing the shell of the coconut is to heat the drained coconut in the oven at 350° for 30 minutes. The shell will crack, making it easier to remove; however, it may still be necessary to tap lightly with a hammer to complete the cracking of the shell.

Depending upon how the coconut is used, the brown tissue covering the meat may or may not be removed. For all-white coconut, use a vegetable parer or a sharp knife to remove the brown covering. To shred coconut, cut the peeled meat into small cubes and grate, using an electric blender, a shredder attachment of an electric mixer, or a hand shredder.

*How to use:* Both the milk and the meat of the coconut can be used as a beverage, as a cooking ingredient, and for eating.

Although milk drained from the ripe coconut can be drunk, it is quite thin and watery. A thicker, and more palatable milk, sometimes used in Latin American and Polynesian cookery, can be made at home by squeezing freshly grated coconut through cheesecloth to extract the milk. Or, the grated coconut can be heated with cow's milk, simmered over low heat until the mixture begins to foam, and then strained. This milk can be chilled and served as a beverage or used in cooking.

Coconut meat is often eaten out-of-hand as a confection or grated for use in baked products. A popular ingredient in candy-making, coconut is also used extensively in salads, pies, cakes, cookies, ice creams, and many fruit desserts. An attractive garnish, coconut is easily minted, tinted, or toasted for use as a dessert topper.

---

### How to tint or toast coconut

Tinted Coconut: Add a few drops of food coloring to grated or shredded coconut in a screw-top jar. Cover and shake vigorously until all the coconut is evenly colored.

Toasted Coconut: Spread a thin layer of grated or shredded coconut in a shallow baking pan. Toast in the oven at 350° till lightly browned, about 6 to 7 minutes. Shake pan or stir often during toasting to insure even toasting of coconut.

---

Canned coconut chips which have been toasted and salted are convenient for sprinkling over desserts such as puddings, ice creams, or fresh fruit cups. Crisp and crunchy, they are delicious when served on a snack tray or combined with mixed nuts. If desired, coconut chips can be made at home from a fresh coconut by thinly slicing the coconut meat into short strips, using a vegetable parer. Toast the coconut strips in the oven as for grated coconut, except sprinkle lightly with salt.

## Apricot-Coconut Ring

1 30-ounce can apricot halves
3 tablespoons butter or margarine
1/3 cup brown sugar
2/3 cup flaked coconut
1 package 1-layer-size white cake mix
2 tablespoons brown sugar
1 tablespoon cornstarch

Drain apricots; reserve syrup. In saucepan heat butter, 3 tablespoons syrup, and 1/3 cup brown sugar till butter melts and sugar dissolves. Pour into greased 5 1/2-cup ring mold. Sprinkle with coconut. Prepare cake mix according to label directions; spoon over coconut. Bake at 350° till cake tests done, about 25 minutes. Cool for 1 minute; invert on serving plate. Remove ring mold. Pile apricots in center.

To prepare glaze, mix 2 tablespoons brown sugar with cornstarch in saucepan. Add remaining apricot syrup. Bring to boiling. Cook, stirring constantly, till thick and clear. Spoon glaze over cake and apricots. Serves 6 to 8.

## Toasted Coconut Ice Cream

In saucepan cook one 14 1/2-ounce can evaporated milk and 1/2 cup sugar till sugar dissolves. Cool; stir in 2 teaspoons vanilla. Pour into 11x 7x1 1/2-inch baking pan. Freeze till firm. Place in a cold bowl, breaking mixture into chunks. Beat smooth with electric or rotary beater. Whip 1 cup whipping cream. Fold whipped cream and 2/3 cup toasted coconut into mixture. Return to pan; cover, and freeze. Serves 8.

## Minted Coconut

In screw-top jar combine 1 teaspoon water, 6 drops green food coloring (optional), and 4 drops peppermint extract. Add one 3 1/2-ounce can flaked coconut. Cover; shake till mixed.

## *A cream pie classic*

Sprinkle coconut liberally over meringue→ just before Coconut Cream Pie goes into the oven. Coconut toasts while top browns.

## Coconut Diamonds

*Chewy, brown sugar topping adds richness—*

6 tablespoons butter, softened
¼ cup granulated sugar
¼ teaspoon salt
1 cup sifted all-purpose flour
• • •
2 eggs
1 teaspoon vanilla
1 cup brown sugar
2 tablespoons all-purpose flour
½ teaspoon salt
1 cup flaked coconut
½ cup coarsely chopped walnuts

Cream together softened butter, ¼ cup granulated sugar, and ¼ teaspoon salt till light and fluffy. Stir in 1 cup flour. Pat mixture into bottom of 9x9x2-inch pan. Bake at 350° till lightly browned, about 15 minutes.

Meanwhile, beat eggs slightly; add vanilla. Gradually add brown sugar, beating just till blended. Stir in 2 tablespoons flour and ½ teaspoon salt. Add flaked coconut and chopped walnuts; mix well. Spread mixture over baked layer. Return to oven and bake 20 minutes longer or till wooden pick comes out clean. Cool. Cut in diamonds. Makes 1½ dozen.

## Coffee-Coconut Ice Cream Balls

*Frozen ice cream balls make a quick dessert—*

Vanilla ice cream
1½ teaspoons instant coffee powder
1½ teaspoons water
1 3½-ounce can flaked coconut
(1⅓ cups)
Chocolate sauce

Chill cookie sheet in freezer. Place scoops of ice cream on chilled cookie sheet; freeze.

Meanwhile, in screw-top jar combine instant coffee powder, water, and flaked coconut. Cover; shake till well mixed.

Remove frozen ice cream balls from freezer. Roll in coffee-coconut mixture. Return to freezer. Store frozen ice cream balls in clear plastic bag in freezer till ready to use.

To serve, place ice cream balls in sherbets. Top dessert with chocolate sauce.

## Coconut-Oatmeal Cookies

2 cups quick-cooking rolled oats
⅔ cup flaked coconut
• • •
1 cup butter or margarine,
softened
1 cup sugar
2 eggs
3 tablespoons milk
1½ teaspoons vanilla
1½ cups sifted all-purpose flour
½ teaspoon baking soda
½ teaspoon salt
• • •
Sugar
Flaked coconut

In shallow baking pan combine oats and ⅔ cup coconut. Toast in the oven at 350° till lightly browned, about 6 to 7 minutes. Shake pan or stir often to insure even browning.

Cream butter with 1 cup sugar till fluffy. Add eggs, milk, and vanilla; beat well. Sift together flour, baking soda, and salt; add to creamed mixture, blending well. Stir in toasted coconut-oat mixture. Drop from teaspoon, 2 inches apart, on *ungreased* cookie sheet.

Flatten with a tumbler dipped in sugar. Sprinkle tops with untoasted flaked coconut. Bake at 400° for 8 to 10 minutes. Remove at once from pan; cool. Makes 4 dozen.

Puncture "eyes" of coconut with ice pick to drain milk. If a thicker milk is desired, squeeze meat of coconut to extract liquid.

## Coconut Cream Pie

    ¾ cup sugar
    ⅓ cup all-purpose flour *or*
        3 tablespoons cornstarch
    2 cups milk
    3 slightly beaten egg yolks
    2 tablespoons butter or margarine
    1 teaspoon vanilla
    1 cup flaked or shredded coconut
    1 *baked* 9-inch pastry shell, cooled
        Meringue
    ⅓ cup flaked or shredded coconut

Combine sugar, flour, and ¼ teaspoon salt. Gradually stir in milk, mixing well. Cook and stir over medium heat till thickened and bubbly. Cook 2 minutes more. Remove from heat. Stir small amount hot mixture into egg yolks; immediately return to hot mixture. Cook and stir 2 minutes. Remove from heat. Add butter, vanilla, and 1 cup coconut. Pour the mixture into the 9-inch cooled pastry shell.

Spread Meringue atop hot filling, sealing to edge of pastry. Sprinkle Meringue with the ⅓ cup coconut. Bake at 350° till golden brown, about 12 to 15 minutes. Cool.

*Meringue:* Beat 3 egg whites with ½ teaspoon vanilla and ¼ teaspoon cream of tartar till soft peaks form. Gradually add 6 tablespoons sugar, beating till stiff peaks form and all sugar is dissolved. Spread the meringue atop the pie.

Crisp and lightly browned, coconut chips add crunch and glamour to desserts when sprinkled over fruit, ice cream, or sherbet.

There's no need to frost this Pineapple Crunch Cake; the coconut-brown sugar topping is spread on the cake before baking.

## Pineapple Crunch Cake

    1 8¾-ounce can crushed pineapple
        (1 cup)
    ⅓ cup shortening
    ½ cup granulated sugar
    1 teaspoon vanilla
    1 egg
    1½ cups sifted all-purpose flour
    1½ teaspoons baking powder
    ¼ teaspoon salt
    ½ cup flaked coconut
    ⅓ cup brown sugar
    ⅓ cup chopped walnuts
    3 tablespoons butter or margarine,
        melted

Drain pineapple *thoroughly*, reserving ½ cup syrup. Thoroughly cream shortening, granulated sugar, and vanilla. Add egg; beat well. Sift together dry ingredients; add to creamed mixture alternately with reserved syrup, beating after each addition. Spread *half* of the batter evenly in greased and floured 8x1½-inch cake pan; spoon pineapple over. Cover with remaining batter. Combine coconut, brown sugar, walnuts, and butter; sprinkle over batter. Bake at 350° till done, about 35 to 40 minutes. Serve warm with ice cream, if desired.

**COD** – A lean, saltwater fish found in North Atlantic waters. Relatives of the cod are found in North Pacific waters and colder regions of the Southern Hemisphere, but their commercial value is of little significance. Cod is of great economic importance to New England, Newfoundland, Norway, and Iceland.

The average cod weighs about ten pounds and grows to a length of three feet; some, however, weigh over 100 pounds and attain a length of five feet. Although their color varies, they are generally olive green on top with darker spots and white on the underside, and with a conspicuous white lateral line along the side.

The natural habitat of cod is near the bottom of the sea where it preys upon nearly all other fish except sharks.

Much of the cod catch is split, dried, and salted on the vessel immediately after it is caught. It is sold flaked, shredded, pickled, smoked, or unsmoked. Unsalted cod is available in frozen fillets in most inland areas, while fresh cod is most plentiful near the source of supply. Fresh or frozen fillets are cooked in much the same manner as ocean perch or haddock. The liver of cod is used commercially in making cod liver oil. (See also *Fish*.)

## Codfish Balls

½ pound salt-cod
3 cups diced, peeled, raw
   potatoes
1 beaten egg
2 tablespoons butter or margarine
   Fat for frying

Soak cod in water several hours or overnight. Drain and dice. Cook potatoes and cod in boiling water till potatoes are tender; drain. Beat with electric mixer. Add egg, butter, and ¼ teaspoon pepper; beat well. Drop by heaping tablespoons (size of golf balls) into deep, hot fat (375°). Fry till golden brown, 2 to 3 minutes; turn once. Drain. Makes 30.

**CODDLE** – To gently cook food in water just below the boiling point. Eggs in the shell are often cooked in this manner.

**COFFEE** – 1. A beverage made from the ground and roasted seeds of a tall, tropical plant. 2. The seeds, green or roasted which are ground and used to make the beverage.

The bean and the beverage have a history as varied as their uses. The little bean has been banned, blessed, and smuggled. To some people, coffee is simply a leisure-time drink; to others it is a means of economic livelihood. But, whatever, from the time of its discovery, coffee has led the world a merry dance.

According to legend, it all began when a Mediterranean goatherd, Kaldi, tasted the bean of a wild cherry after the fashion of his frisky goats. When he, too, became pepped-up, he reported his find to his local priest who dipped the bean in hot water and drank the unsweetened brew. From then on, the monks drank coffee to help them through long ceremonies.

The church, in fact, has done a great deal to promote the spread of coffee. When Mohammedan priests realized that Turkish villagers were spending the mandatory hour of daily prayer gossiping over a cup of coffee, they declared the brew alcohol, forbidden by the *Koran,* and banned it.

Not to be outdone, Pope Clementine VII accepted that what was bad for the Mohammedans was good for the Christians and promptly blessed the bean into the church, thus popularizing the beverage.

Later, during the Crusades, when the Austrian army was driving the Turkish forces from the Holy Land, an Austrian soldier, Franz George Kolschitzky, was rewarded for his heroics with all the Turkish coffee that was left behind after the expulsion. With this large supply he started a coffee shop in Vienna.

Before long, the idea of coffee shops spread across the European continent. Men would spend afternoons in these coffee emporiums, discussing the politics of the day. In fact, it was in such a shop, Boston's Green Dragon Coffeehouse, that the Boston Tea Party was planned.

The establishment of the coffee break would seem to be a natural extension of the British tea break, but this is not the case. It stemmed from the coffeehouse idea. The officers of the old Mississippi Steamship Line in New Orleans decided in

1930 that the Brazilian tradition of breaking for coffee in the morning and in the afternoon had multiple benefits to the company—psychologically and economically.

Initially, the major supply of coffee was grown in Java. This was until a Franciscan monk, Father Villase, who wished to aid his poor parishioners, smuggled the closely guarded plant out of Java and into Rio de Janeiro where he planted it in the monastery gardens. From this improbable beginning stems the domination of Brazil as a grower and exporter of coffee.

In the early years of colonial America, coffee was purchased green, then roasted at home. Then, in 1790, a New York businessman opened the first coffee-roasting plant. Here the beans were roasted over a slow coal fire and crudely packaged in newspaper for retail sale. Although such commercial roasting was not readily accepted, inventors persisted in the development of better roasting machines.

The first ground and roasted coffee appeared on the New York market in the early 1860s. Methods of packaging improved within the next few years. In 1900, the first vacuum-packed coffee appeared on the market, thereby providing coffee that retained its aromatic qualities.

*How coffee is produced:* Coffee trees grow best in a well-watered, tropical climate, preferably at a high altitude, and under a constant temperature of 65 to 70 degrees. Because of these conditions, it is not possible to grow coffee in the United States, except for a small amount of Kona coffee grown in Hawaii. The major coffee growing countries are Brazil, El Savador, Columbia, Costa Rica, Guatemala, Arabia, India, Java, and Malaya.

The coffee tree, which doesn't mature for about five years, is shrublike and bears a fruit known as cherries. When ripe, these cherries are red; however, the plant often bears blossoms and green and red cherries at the same time. Consequently, the cherries must be hand-picked.

Each cherry has two coffee beans in its center. Once the beans are removed, the pulp of the cherry is discarded. The first step in production of coffee after cleaning involves the blending of various types of

Use one package of pudding to make two coffee-flavored desserts—Chocolate Almond Cups and Mocha Marshmallow Pudding.

beans. After the correct blend is achieved, the beans are carefully roasted to develop a characteristic flavor and color. During roasting, the bean "pops" and increases to nearly twice its size.

Mechanization has greatly reduced the possibility of damage to the coffee bean that was once of great concern to the roasters. The individual coffee beans are loaded onto large hoppers from which a large number of blends can be made. These blends are computer selected to ensure that the coffee is clean and the blend is roasted at the right temperature—generally at 360° for 15 minutes. Different degrees of roasting produce different flavors of coffee. Names of different roasts include cinnamon, high, New York, Chicago, New Orleans, French, and Italian.

Coffee can be brewed from the whole, roasted bean, but a quicker and more flavorful cup of coffee is prepared from ground beans. Although of no nutritional value, tannins are responsible for much of the characteristic flavor of coffee. Desirable in small amounts, too much tannin results in a bitter-flavored coffee.

Various commercial grinds of coffee are made for use in different types of coffee makers. Home-type coffee grinders are still popular in some homes despite the fact that the grind is generally not as uniform as that ground commercially.

After grinding, the coffee is vacuum-packed to prevent staling, thus insuring maximum retention of the aromatic oils. The sudden, rich aroma and pressure release which accompanies the opening of a vacuum-packed can of coffee is due to carbon dioxide given off by the coffee within the can after it is packed.

*Nutritional value:* Coffee contains caffein which acts as a mild stimulant to the body. For people who wish to avoid caffein, decaffeinated coffee is available in which most of the caffein has been removed.

A few minerals and a substance which is converted to the B vitamin, niacin, are present in coffee but in very small amounts. A pleasant beverage, coffee, when served with a meal, enhances the enjoyment of other foods rather than contributing important nutrients to the diet.

*Types of coffee:* Over 100 different kinds of coffee, each with its own flavor, are found throughout the world. Unlike so many other foods, there is no "best" coffee, although each nation has its favorite. Italians and French are more accustomed to a heavy or dark-roast coffee while Americans prefer a medium-roast coffee. Even within the United States, a variation in coffee preferences exists. Along the West Coast, coffee is lightly roasted, is light in color, and has a sharp flavor. Moving eastward, it gets progressively darker. Coffee is darkest around New York, but it is also very dark in the South where it is often blended with chicory. Most brands found on the market today are a blend of several coffees which accounts for numerous flavor variations.

A major boon to the coffee industry was the development of instant coffee. This offers a much easier-to-prepare cup of coffee and, to many people, an equally satisfying drink. To manufacture this product, roasted, ground coffee is brewed with water. The grounds are discarded and the coffee brew is dried. The powder which remains after drying is packaged and sold as instant coffee. A somewhat different procedure is used to make freeze-dried coffee. This coffee brew is first frozen, then the moisture is removed in a vacuum, producing dry, brittle crystals of coffee which dissolve readily in water.

*How to select:* Personal preference determines whether regular, instant, freeze-dried, or decaffeinated coffee is purchased. If regular coffee is used, however, the grind should be selected on the basis of the method used to prepare the coffee.

Regular grind is best suited for steeped or percolator coffee, drip grind for drip coffee, and fine grind for vacuum coffee. A more recent development is a special grind designed for use in electric percolators. As a rule, it is best to use the finest grind of coffee possible for the particular method of coffee making, as this allows a greater surface area of the coffee to be exposed to the water. Thus, a richer, more full-bodied flavor results in the beverage.

*How to store:* Exposing ground coffee to the air causes staling which in turn produces a weaker flavored coffee. After opening, coffee retains its freshness best when stored in the refrigerator or freezer in a tightly covered container. To avoid long storage, purchase coffee in amounts which will be used within a short time.

*How to use:* Coffee is served most often either plain or with cream and/or sugar. Combined with other ingredients, it serves as the basis for many special drinks such as café au lait, café brûlot, and Irish coffee. The roasted coffee bean is also used as an ingredient in a wide variety of desserts. Added either in dry form, as instant coffee powder, or in liquid form, the strong flavor of coffee blends very well with chocolate, butterscotch and a multitude of other spices. (See also *Beverage*.)

---

### How to make coffee

Start with a clean coffee maker. Clean well after each use to remove oils that collect.

Use fresh, cold water for making coffee. Measure accurately. Allow 2 level measuring tablespoons coffee (or 1 coffee measure) for each ¾ cup standard measuring cup water. Proportions may vary with individual taste, brand of coffee, and coffee maker.

For best results, use the full capacity of coffee maker and never boil coffee.

Accurate timing is important. Find the best timing, then stick to it.

**Automatic Coffee:** Follow the directions given by manufacturer.

**Percolator Coffee:** Measure cold water into percolator. Measure coffee into basket. Cover; place over heat. Bring to boiling; reduce heat. Perk *gently* 6 to 8 minutes. Remove basket; keep hot over *very low heat.*

**Vacuum Coffee:** Measure cold water into lower bowl; place over heat. Insert filter and correct measure of finely ground coffee in upper bowl. When water boils, insert upper bowl into lower bowl. When water rises to top, stir mixture. Reduce heat. After 2 or 3 minutes, remove from heat. Let coffee return to lower bowl before removing upper bowl.

**Drip Coffee:** Bring cold water to boiling. Measure coffee into coffee basket; pour boiling water in top water container. Let drip through coffee. Remove basket and water container and stir briskly.

**Instant Coffee:** For each cup place 1 rounded teaspoon instant coffee powder and ¾ cup boiling water into coffeepot. Heat over *low* heat 5 minutes. Or, prepare in cup.

To prepare coffee over an open fire, measure water plus a little extra to make up for that which boils away. Bring to a hard, rolling boil. Add 1 heaping tablespoon coffee for each cup water. Boil 1 minute, then set off coals but close enough to fire to keep hot.

To prepare iced coffee, brew coffee using *half* the amount of water for the usual amount of coffee. Pour hot coffee into ice-filled tumblers. *Or*, dissolve two rounded teaspoons instant coffee powder in one-half glass cold water; add ice and stir well.

Capped with whipped cream and spicy gingersnap crumbs, Coffee-Chiffon Torte is the perfect ending for an elegant meal.

## Chocolate Coffee

    1 cup water
    2 1-ounce squares unsweetened
        chocolate
    ¼ cup sugar
    2 tablespoons instant coffee
        powder
      Dash salt
            •   •   •
    3 cups milk
      Whipped cream

In saucepan combine water, chocolate, sugar, instant coffee powder, and salt; stir over low heat just till chocolate melts.

Gradually add milk to chocolate mixture, stirring constantly. When piping hot, *but not boiling*, remove mixture from heat and beat with rotary beater till frothy.

To serve, pour chocolate coffee into cups or mugs. Spoon a dollop of whipped cream atop each serving. Makes 6 servings.

## Swedish Egg Coffee

In small bowl combine 1 slightly beaten egg (reserve shell) and ⅔ cup coffee. (If stronger coffee is desired, use 1 cup coffee.) Add ½ cup cold water; blend well. Stir in crumbled egg shell. Add to 8 cups boiling water.

Heat and stir over high heat till foam disappears, about 4 minutes. Remove from heat; cover. Let settle for about 7 to 10 minutes. Serve clear coffee off top, or strain through fine mesh strainer. Makes 10 servings.

## Café Aruba

    3 cups hot double-strength coffee
    ¼ cup orange peel cut in very thin
        strips
    1 orange, peeled and sliced
    1 tablespoon sugar
    1 teaspoon aromatic bitters
    ½ cup whipping cream

Measure hot coffee into glass pot. Add orange peel and slices. Let mixture steep over low heat for 15 minutes. Add sugar and bitters. *Do not boil.* Strain; pour into warmed glasses or mugs. Whip cream; sweeten to taste, if desired. Spoon atop coffee. Serves 4 or 5.

## Cool Coffee Eggnog

    4 cups milk
    2 beaten egg yolks
    ¼ cup sugar
    2 tablespoons instant coffee
        powder
    1 teaspoon vanilla
    ¼ teaspoon salt
            •   •   •
    2 egg whites
    3 tablespoons sugar

In medium saucepan stir milk into beaten egg yolks. Add ¼ cup sugar, instant coffee powder, vanilla, and salt. Cook over medium heat, stirring constantly, till mixture coats a metal spoon. Remove from heat and chill.

Just before serving, beat egg whites till foamy. Gradually add 3 tablespoons sugar, beating to soft peaks. Add to chilled coffee mixture; mix thoroughly. Makes 6 to 8 servings.

## Spiced Iced Coffee

    2 tablespoons sugar
    2 tablespoons instant coffee
      powder
  1/4 teaspoon ground cinnamon
1 1/2 cups milk
    2 cups cola beverage, chilled

Combine sugar, instant coffee powder, and ground cinnamon. Stir in milk. Blend in blender or with rotary beater till well mixed. Add cola; stir gently just till combined. Pour into ice-filled tumblers. Makes 6 servings.

## Brazilian Float

In saucepan heat together one 1-ounce square unsweetened chocolate and 2 tablespoons sugar till chocolate melts and sugar dissolves. Remove from heat. Stir in 1/2 cup strong hot coffee. Add 2 cups hot milk; mix well. Chill. Scoop 1 pint vanilla ice cream into 4 glasses; add chocolate mixture and stir. Serves 4.

## Almond-Coffee Tortoni

*A dessert to have on hand for unexpected guests—*

  1/2 cup whipping cream
    2 tablespoons sugar
  1/2 teaspoon vanilla
    2 drops almond extract
      . . .
    1 egg white
    2 tablespoons sugar
      . . .
    2 tablespoons finely chopped
      almonds, toasted
    2 tablespoons coconut, toasted
  1/2 teaspoon instant coffee powder

In small mixing bowl whip cream with 2 tablespoons sugar, vanilla, and almond extract. Beat egg white to soft peaks. Gradually add 2 tablespoons sugar; beat to stiff peaks.

Mix toasted almonds and coconut. Fold beaten egg white, almond-coconut mixture, and instant coffee powder into whipped cream. Spoon dessert mixture into 4 paper bake cups in muffin pan. Sprinkle remaining nut mixture over all. Freeze till firm. Makes 4 servings.

## Coffee Chiffon Torte

*Spicy gingersnaps add crunch—*

    2 envelopes (2 tablespoons)
      unflavored gelatin
  1/2 cup sugar
  1/2 teaspoon salt
    4 teaspoons instant coffee powder
    3 cups milk
    3 beaten egg yolks
    3 egg whites
    1 teaspoon vanilla
  1/4 teaspoon cream of tartar
    4 gingersnaps, crushed (1/3 cup)
      Whipped cream

In saucepan mix gelatin, sugar, salt, and coffee powder. Combine milk and beaten egg yolks. Add to gelatin mixture. Cook and stir till gelatin and sugar dissolve and mixture thickens slightly. Chill till partially set.

Beat together egg whites, vanilla, and cream of tartar till soft peaks form. Fold in gelatin mixture. Chill till mixture mounds.

Spoon mixture into 6 1/2-cup mold. Chill till firm. Unmold onto serving dish. At serving time, sprinkle mold with *half* the gingersnap crumbs. Spoon whipped cream atop mold; garnish with remaining crumbs. Makes 8 servings.

## Mocha-Marshmallow Pudding and Chocolate-Almond Cups

    1 6 3/4-ounce package *instant*
      chocolate pudding mix
    2 tablespoons sugar
    1 tablespoon instant coffee
      powder
  1/2 cup miniature marshmallows
    2 tablespoons chopped
      almonds, toasted

Prepare pudding according to package directions, adding sugar and coffee powder to dry mix. Divide mixture in half. *Mocha-Marshmallow Pudding:* To *half* the pudding mixture, add marshmallows. Pile in 4 sherbets. Makes 4 servings. *Chocolate-Almond Cups:* To remaining *half* of the pudding mixture, add almonds. Spoon into 4 foil or paper bake cups in muffin pans. Freeze. Remove desserts from muffin pan; wrap, and return to freezer. Serves 4.

## Kona Coffee Torte

*A delectable dessert with an orange filling—*

Cake:
- 1½ tablespoons instant coffee powder
- 6 egg yolks
- 2 cups granulated sugar
- 2 cups sifted all-purpose flour
- 3 teaspoons baking powder
- 1 teaspoon vanilla
- 1 cup ground walnuts
- 6 stiff-beaten egg whites

Orange Filling:
- 1 cup butter, softened
- 2 cups sifted confectioners' sugar
- 2 teaspoons unsweetened cocoa powder
- ½ teaspoon instant coffee powder
- 2 tablespoons orange juice

Mocha Frosting:
- 2 cups sifted confectioners' sugar
- 2 teaspoons unsweetened cocoa powder
- ½ teaspoon instant coffee powder
- 3 tablespoons butter, melted
- ½ teaspoon vanilla

*Cake:* Dissolve 1½ tablespoons coffee powder in 1 cup cold water. Beat egg yolks till light and fluffy. Gradually add granulated sugar, beating till thick. Sift together flour, baking powder, and ¼ teaspoon salt. Add to yolks alternately with dissolved coffee; beat well after each addition. Add 1 teaspoon vanilla and nuts. Fold in stiff-beaten egg whites.

Bake in 3 paper-lined 9x1½-inch round cake pans at 325° for 30 minutes. Cool 10 minutes. Remove from pans; cool. Fill cake with Orange Filling; frost top with Mocha Frosting.

*Orange Filling:* Cream 1 cup softened butter with 2 cups sifted confectioners' sugar. Beat in 2 teaspoons unsweetened cocoa powder, ½ teaspoon instant coffee powder, 2 tablespoons cold water, and orange juice.

*Mocha Frosting:* Mix 2 cups sifted confectioners' sugar, 2 teaspoons unsweetened cocoa powder, and ½ teaspoon instant coffee powder. Add 2 tablespoons cold water; 3 tablespoons butter, melted; and ½ teaspoon vanilla. Beat till frosting is of spreading consistency.

## Ice Cream Sundae Mold

- ¼ cup flaked coconut, toasted
- 1½ teaspoons brandy flavoring
- 1 quart vanilla ice cream, softened
- ¼ cup slivered almonds, toasted
- 1 quart coffee ice cream, softened
- Fudgy Chocolate Sauce

Stir coconut and brandy flavoring into vanilla ice cream; turn into 6½-cup mold. Freeze till firm. Stir almonds into coffee ice cream; spoon into mold atop frozen vanilla layer. Freeze firm, about 5 hours. Unmold. Drizzle with Fudgy Chocolate Sauce; sprinkle with additional toasted almonds, if desired. Pass remaining sauce. Makes 10 to 12 servings.

*Fudgy Chocolate Sauce:* In saucepan combine one 6-ounce package semisweet chocolate pieces and ⅔ cup light corn syrup; stir over low heat till chocolate melts. Cool. Blend in one 6-ounce can evaporated milk (⅔ cup).

## Coffee Chiffon Pie

- ⅓ cup sugar
- 1 envelope (1 tablespoon) unflavored gelatin
- 1 tablespoon instant coffee powder
- ¼ teaspoon ground nutmeg
- 3 slightly beaten egg yolks
- 1 14½-ounce can evaporated milk
- ½ teaspoon vanilla
- 3 egg whites
- ⅓ cup sugar
- 1 *baked* 9-inch pastry shell (See *Pastry*)
- ½ cup whipping cream

In saucepan combine first 4 ingredients and dash salt. Combine egg yolks and evaporated milk; stir into gelatin mixture. Cook and stir till gelatin dissolves and mixture thickens slightly. Stir in vanilla. Chill till partially set, stirring often. Beat smooth.

Beat egg whites to soft peaks; gradually add ⅓ cup sugar, beating to stiff peaks. Fold in gelatin mixture. Pile in baked pastry shell. Chill till firm. Whip cream. Top pie with whipped cream and chocolate curls, if desired.

A dessert to top all desserts—Ice Cream Sundae Mold. Fudgy Chocolate Sauce flows generously down layers of coffee and vanilla ice cream studded with toasted almonds and coconut.

## Coffee Angel Pie

    2 egg whites
    ½ teaspoon vanilla
    ¼ teaspoon salt
    ¼ teaspoon cream of tartar
    ½ cup sugar
    ½ cup finely chopped pecans
    1 pint coffee ice cream
    1 pint vanilla ice cream

        •   •   •

        **Caramel-Raisin Sauce**

Beat together egg whites, vanilla, salt, and cream of tartar till soft peaks form. Gradually beat in sugar till very stiff peaks form and sugar is dissolved. Fold in pecans. Spread in well-buttered 9-inch pie plate, building up sides to form a shell. Bake at 275° for 1 hour. Turn off heat; let dry in oven, with door closed, for 1 hour. Remove from oven; cool.

Pile scoops of coffee and vanilla ice cream into cooled shell; freeze till firm. Let pie stand 20 minutes at room temperature before serving. Cut in wedges to serve.

Serve with *Caramel-Raisin Sauce:* In small saucepan melt 3 tablespoons butter or margarine; stir in 1 cup brown sugar, 1 6-ounce can evaporated milk (⅔ cup), and dash salt. Cook over medium-low heat, stirring constantly, till sugar dissolves and mixture boils. Remove from heat; stir in ½ cup golden raisins and 1 teaspoon vanilla. Cool sauce slightly. Spoon over pie. Makes 1⅓ cups sauce.

**COFFEE CAKE, COFFEE BREAD**—Rich, sweet cake or bread served at breakfast, brunch, or the mid-morning coffee break, rather than as a dessert.

There are two types of coffee cake. One type resembles bread because it's made with yeast; the other is more like cake because of the leavening effect on the batter by the baking powder or baking soda. Both types are enriched with eggs or egg yolks and sweetened with sugar. In addition, fruits, nuts, and spices, such as cinnamon and nutmeg, are used to flavor the dough, filling, or topping.

Coffee cakes are shaped in many different designs. The dough can be arranged in pinwheels, sunburst circles, braids, and Christmas trees. The shape can also be formed by baking in loaf, oblong, square, round, and tube or bundt pans.

Toppings make a coffee cake more attractive and appealing. Confectioners' icing is frequently drizzled over the warm bread. Nuts, candied fruit, raisins, and streusel topping can be sprinkled over the top for variety in flavor, appearance, and texture.

Coffee cake is usually served warm from the oven in the morning. Its addition to a mid-morning coffee break or coffee klatch completes the affair whether the gathering is formal or informal. A hot bread is a must for brunch menus, and coffee cakes are favorites with both the hostess and guests. At breakfast, these sweet, hot breads make the simplest menu seem glamorous. A menu of bacon or Canadian-style bacon, eggs, cups of piping-hot coffee, and a fruit with the coffee cake will make a weekend breakfast special, dress up a family breakfast, or impress company.

*How to prepare with convenience products:* Both the bread- and cake-type coffee cakes can be made using convenience products. Biscuit and hot roll mix form the foundation with fruit, nuts, and spices added for flavoring. Other mixes, for instance muffin mixes, already have much of the flavoring and only require minor adaptation. Refrigerated biscuits and rolls are probably the quickest and easiest convenience products to use. They can be dipped in melted butter, sugar and spices, and nuts, or filled with a favorite fruit mixture.

## Miniature Brunch Loaf

      2 tablespoons chopped pecans
      3 tablespoons brown sugar
      1 cup packaged biscuit mix
    ¼ teaspoon ground cinnamon
    ⅛ teaspoon ground mace
              •   •   •
      3 tablespoons milk
      1 egg
      2 tablespoons butter, melted
    ¼ teaspoon vanilla

Mix pecans with *2 tablespoons* brown sugar; set aside. Combine the biscuit mix, remaining brown sugar, cinnamon, and mace. Combine milk, egg, *1 tablespoon* of the melted butter, and vanilla. Make a well in the center of dry ingredients; add liquid all at once.

Stir with fork till blended. Spoon *half* of the biscuit mixture into greased 5½x3x2¼-inch loaf pan; brush with *some* of the remaining butter and sprinkle with *half* of the pecan mixture. Repeat with remainder of the biscuit mixture, butter, and pecans. Bake at 350° for 25 to 30 minutes. Serve warm.

## Pear-Berry Coffee Cake

      3 fresh pears, peeled and cored
      1 teaspoon lemon juice
    ½ cup brown sugar
    ½ cup sifted all-purpose flour
    ¼ teaspoon ground nutmeg
    ¼ cup butter or margarine
      1 13½-ounce package blueberry
          muffin mix

Slice pears lengthwise into eighths. Sprinkle with lemon juice. Mix sugar, flour, and nutmeg together; cut in butter. Prepare muffin mix according to package directions. Turn into greased 9x9x2-inch pan. Top with pears. Spoon crumbly mixture over. Bake at 400° about 35 minutes. Makes 9 servings.

## *Visions of sugarplums*

Studded with almonds and cherries and→ drizzled with rich syrup, Sugarplum Ring makes a welcome gift or highlights a brunch.

## Prune-Nut Braid

1 13¾-ounce package hot roll mix
2 tablespoons butter or margarine, melted and cooled
1 teaspoon grated orange peel
¾ cup canned prune filling
¼ cup chopped pecans
   Confectioners' Icing

Prepare hot roll mix according to package directions. Add butter or margarine and orange peel; mix well. Cover; let rise in warm place till doubled, about 1 hour. On lightly floured surface, knead dough about 1 minute. Roll dough to a 12-inch square. Cut into 3 strips.

Spread ¼ cup prune filling down center of each strip. Sprinkle evenly with nuts. Pinch dough up around filling to form 3 ropes. Place on greased baking sheet and braid dough; pinch ends together. Cover and let rise till almost doubled, about 40 minutes. Bake at 375° till done about 25 minutes. Glaze while warm with confectioners' icing and decorate with red sugar and pecans, if desired. Serve warm.

*Confectioners' Icing:* Combine 1 cup confectioners' sugar, 1 to 1½ tablespoons milk, and ¼ teaspoon vanilla. Mix till smooth.

Serve a gala breakfast on even the busiest mornings by using refrigerated rolls to make a ring of Quick Apple Pinwheels.

## Quick Apple Pinwheels

1 8-ounce package refrigerated crescent rolls (8 rolls)
1 medium apple, cored, peeled, and chopped (about 1 cup)
¼ cup raisins
2 tablespoons granulated sugar
½ teaspoon grated lemon peel
   Dash ground nutmeg
   Milk
1 tablespoon brown sugar

Separate crescent rolls. On greased baking sheet, arrange triangles, bases overlapping, in complete circle. (Center of circle should be *open*, with points toward *outside*.) Combine apple, raisins, granulated sugar, lemon peel, and nutmeg. Spoon apple filling mixture over bases of triangles. Fold points over filling, tucking points under bases of triangles at center circle. Brush with a little milk; sprinkle with brown sugar. Bake at 350° till golden brown, about 25 minutes.

***How to prepare using the quick method:*** Coffee cakes made by the quick method use baking powder or baking soda for leavening and are not kneaded. Resembling cake more than bread in texture, they may have a more open grain and uneven surface than coffee cakes made with yeast. This method, however, takes much less time and work. The coffee cake can be mixed quickly and baked in time for breakfast or served to unexpected guests.

## Coffee Cake

Combine ¼ cup salad oil, 1 beaten egg, and ½ cup milk. Sift together 1½ cups sifted all-purpose flour, ¾ cup granulated sugar, 2 teaspoons baking powder, and ½ teaspoon salt. Add dry ingredients to milk mixture; mix well. Pour into greased 9x9x2-inch pan.

Combine ¼ cup brown sugar, 1 tablespoon all-purpose flour, 1 teaspoon ground cinnamon, 1 tablespoon melted butter or margarine, and ½ cup broken nuts. Sprinkle over batter in pan.

Bake coffee cake at 375° till done, about 25 minutes. Serve cake warm.

## Orange-Date Coffee Cake

        2 cups sifted all-purpose flour
    ½ cup granulated sugar
        3 teaspoons baking powder
    ½ teaspoon salt
        1 slightly beaten egg
    ½ cup milk
    ½ cup salad oil
    ½ cup snipped dates
        2 teaspoons grated orange peel
    ½ cup orange juice
        2 tablespoons butter or mar-
            garine, softened
    ½ cup brown sugar
        1 teaspoon ground cinnamon
    ½ cup chopped walnuts

In large bowl, sift together flour, granulated sugar, baking powder, and salt. Combine egg, milk, and salad oil; add all at once to dry ingredients. Stir just till well blended. Combine dates, orange peel, and orange juice; stir into batter just till blended. Spread batter evenly in greased 11x7x1½-inch baking pan. Combine butter, brown sugar, cinnamon, and nuts. Sprinkle over batter. Bake at 375° for 25 to 30 minutes. Serve warm.

End the search for something different to serve at breakfast or at coffee by baking the lightly spiced Orange-Date Coffee Cake.

## Toasted Coconut Coffee Cake

        3 cups sifted all-purpose flour
        1 cup sugar
        4 teaspoons baking powder
        1 teaspoon salt
        1 3½-ounce can flaked coconut,
            toasted (1⅓ cups)
        2 teaspoons shredded orange peel
        1 slightly beaten egg
    1½ cups milk
        2 tablespoons salad oil
        1 teaspoon vanilla

In mixing bowl, sift together flour, sugar, baking powder, and salt. Stir in toasted coconut and orange peel. Combine egg, milk, oil, and vanilla; add to dry ingredients all at once, stirring just till combined. Turn batter into greased 9x5x3-inch loaf pan. Bake at 350° till done, 60 to 70 minutes. Remove from pan. Cool on rack. Makes 1 loaf.

## Apricot-Almond Coffee Cake

    ¾ cup dried apricots, snipped
        Milk
    ¼ cup shortening
    ¾ cup granulated sugar
        1 egg
    1½ cups sifted all-purpose flour
        2 teaspoons baking powder
    ¾ teaspoon salt
    ½ teaspoon ground cinnamon
    ½ cup brown sugar
    ⅓ cup all-purpose flour
        4 tablespoons butter or margarine
    ⅓ cup chopped almonds

In saucepan, combine apricots and 1 cup water; simmer, uncovered, 15 minutes. Cool. Drain, adding enough milk to liquid to make ½ cup. Cream together shortening and granulated sugar. Add egg and beat well. Sift together the 1½ cups flour, baking powder, salt, and cinnamon. Add to creamed mixture alternately with the milk mixture, beginning and ending with dry ingredients; stir in apricots. Turn into greased 9x1½-inch layer cake pan or 9x9x2-inch baking pan. Combine brown sugar and the ⅓ cup flour; cut in butter or margarine till crumbly; add almonds. Sprinkle over batter. Bake at 350° for 40 to 45 minutes. Serve warm.

## Cowboy Coffee Cake

2½ cups sifted all-purpose flour
2 cups brown sugar
½ teaspoon salt
⅔ cup shortening

• • •

2 teaspoons baking powder
½ teaspoon baking soda
½ teaspoon ground cinnamon
½ teaspoon ground nutmeg
1 cup sour milk
2 beaten eggs

Mix flour, sugar, salt, and shortening till crumbly; reserve ½ cup. To remaining crumbs, add baking powder, baking soda, cinnamon, and nutmeg; mix well. Add sour milk and eggs; mix well. Pour into 2 greased and floured 8x1½-inch round pans; top with reserved ½ cup crumbs. Bake at 375° for 25 to 30 minutes. Serve warm. Makes 2 cakes.

## Banana Coffee Bread

½ cup shortening
1 cup sugar
2 eggs
¾ cup mashed ripe banana

• • •

1¼ cups sifted all-purpose flour
¾ teaspoon baking soda
½ teaspoon salt

Cream shortening and sugar till fluffy. Add eggs, one at a time, beating well after each. Stir in banana. Sift together flour, baking soda, and salt; add to banana mixture. Mix well. Pour into greased 9x9x2-inch pan. Bake at 350° for 30 to 35 minutes.

***How to prepare using yeast method:*** Coffee cakes made with yeast resemble bread but are sweeter and richer. This method takes more time to prepare than the quick method and usually requires kneading. However, the end product, like homemade bread, is well worth all the effort required.

Coffee cakes can be baked and frozen for later use. If the recipe yields two cakes, serve one and freeze the other. Or, make two recipes while all the ingredients, mix-

ing bowls, and utensils are out. Wrap the baked coffee cakes in foil and freeze. Those made with yeast can be stored for as long as six to eight months.

When ready to use, thaw the bread in its wrapper at room temperature allowing about three hours. The bread can also be heated in the foil wrapper at 325° for 15 to 20 minutes to thaw and reheat it at the same time. (See also *Bread.*)

## Sugarplum Ring

1 package active dry yeast
3¾ to 4 cups sifted all-purpose
flour
¾ cup milk
⅓ cup sugar
⅓ cup shortening
1 teaspoon salt
2 beaten eggs

• • •

¼ cup butter or margarine,
melted
¾ cup sugar
1 teaspoon ground cinnamon
½ cup whole blanched almonds
½ cup candied whole red cherries
⅓ cup dark corn syrup

In large mixer bowl, combine yeast and *2 cups* flour. Heat milk, the ⅓ cup sugar, shortening, and salt just till warm, stirring occasionally to melt shortening. Add to dry mixture in mixing bowl; add eggs. Beat at low speed with electric mixer for ½ minute, scraping sides of bowl constantly. Beat 3 minutes at high speed. Stir in by hand enough of the remaining flour to make a soft dough. Mix thoroughly and place in a greased bowl, turning once to grease surface. Cover and let rise till double, about 2 hours. Punch down and let rest 10 minutes.

Divide dough into 4 parts. Cut each part into 10 pieces and shape into balls. Dip balls in the melted butter, then in the ¾ cup sugar blended with the cinnamon. Arrange ⅓ of the balls in well-greased 10-inch tube pan. Sprinkle with some of the almonds and cherries. Repeat with two more layers. Mix corn syrup with butter left from dipping balls; drizzle over top.

Cover and let rise in warm place till double, about 1 hour. Bake at 350° for 35 minutes. Cool 5 minutes; invert pan and remove ring.

## Chocolate Chip Coffee Ring

In large mixer bowl, combine 1 package active dry yeast and 1¼ cups sifted all-purpose flour. Heat together ½ cup milk, ¼ cup butter or margarine, 3 tablespoons sugar, and ½ teaspoon salt just till warm, stirring occasionally to melt butter. Add to dry mixture in bowl; add 1 egg. Beat at low speed of electric mixer for ½ minute, scraping sides of bowl constantly. Beat 3 minutes at high speed. By hand, stir in ½ cup sifted all-purpose flour. Add ½ cup semisweet chocolate pieces; mix well. Turn into well-greased 4½-cup ring mold. Cover; let rise till double, 45 minutes to 1 hour.

Bake at 400° for 12 to 15 minutes. Remove from pan immediately; drizzle with confectioners' sugar icing while warm.

## English Tea Ring

   1 package active dry yeast
   2½ to 2¾ cups sifted all-purpose
        flour
   ¾ cup milk
   ¼ cup sugar
   ¼ cup shortening
   1 beaten egg
   ½ teaspoon vanilla
   ¼ cup sugar
   1 teaspoon ground cinnamon
   ½ cup chopped walnuts
   ½ cup chopped mixed candied
        fruits and peels

In large mixer bowl, combine yeast and 1½ *cups* flour. Heat milk, ¼ cup sugar, shortening, and 1 teaspoon salt just till warm, stirring occasionally to melt shortening. Add to dry mixture; add beaten egg and vanilla. Beat at low speed with electric mixer for ½ minute, scraping sides of bowl constantly. Beat 3 minutes at high speed. By hand, stir in enough of the remaining flour to make a soft dough. Knead lightly on floured surface. Place in a greased bowl; turn once to grease surface. Cover; let rise till double in bulk, 1½ to 2 hours.

Roll to 13x9-inch rectangle, about ¼ inch thick. Brush with melted butter; spread evenly with Fruit Filling. Roll starting from long side, like jelly roll. Seal edge. Shape in a ring on greased baking sheet. With scissors, snip almost to center at 1-inch intervals. Pull sec-

tions apart and twist slightly. Let rise till double, 35 to 45 minutes. Bake in a 375° oven for about 20 to 25 minutes.

*Fruit Filling:* Mix ¼ cup sugar, ground cinnamon, walnuts, and candied fruits.

## Swedish Holiday Braid

   1 package active dry yeast
   5½ to 6 cups sifted all-purpose
        flour
   1½ teaspoons ground cardamom
   ¼ teaspoon ground mace
   1¼ cups milk
   ½ cup sugar
   ½ cup butter, margarine, or
        shortening, softened
   2 beaten eggs
   1 cup dark or light raisins
      Sugar Glaze

In large mixer bowl combine yeast, 2¾ *cups* flour, cardamom, and mace. Heat milk, sugar, butter, and 2 teaspoons salt just till warm, stirring to melt butter. Add to dry mixture; add eggs. Beat at low speed with electric mixer for ½ minute, scraping sides of bowl constantly. Beat 3 minutes at high speed. Add raisins. By hand, stir in enough of the remaining flour to make a soft dough.

Turn out on a lightly floured surface and knead till smooth and elastic, about 8 to 10 minutes. Place in a lightly greased bowl, turning once to grease surface. Cover and let rise in warm place till double in bulk, about 1½ hours. Punch down.

Divide and round the dough into 2 balls, one for each braid. Cover and let rest for 10 minutes. For each braid: divide one ball in thirds. Shape into strands 15 inches long, tapering the ends. Line up the strands 1 inch apart on a lightly greased baking sheet. Braid loosely without stretching the dough, beginning in the middle, and working toward either end. Seal ends well. Repeat with second half.

Cover and let rise in a warm place till double, about 45 minutes. Bake at 350° for about 25 to 30 minutes. While warm, spread with Sugar Glaze. Makes 2 braided loaves.

*Sugar Glaze:* To 1 cup sifted confectioners' sugar, add 2 tablespoons hot water and 1 teaspoon butter or margarine. Mix till well blended. Drizzle over warm braids.

Shaping ropes of dough in a circle forms the Sunburst Coffee Cake design. Raisins, cherries, and citron fill the inside while confectioners' icing and cherry halves garnish the top.

To shape coffee cake: Divide dough into 12 pieces; roll each to form 8-inch ropes. Place 6 ropes, twisted in a U-shape, around 4-inch circle in center of baking sheet.

Form the remaining 6 ropes in O-shapes; join seamed ends at center of circle, allowing rounded end to overlap the first layer of U-shapes at a point in between the petals.

## Sugarplum Loaves

In large mixer bowl, combine 2 packages active dry yeast and 2½ cups sifted all-purpose flour. Heat 1¼ cups milk, ½ cup sugar, ¼ cup shortening, and 1½ teaspoons salt just till warm, stirring occasionally to melt shortening. Add to dry mixture in mixer bowl; add 1 teaspoon grated lemon peel and 2 beaten eggs. Beat at low speed with electric mixer for ½ minute, scraping sides of bowl constantly. Beat 3 minutes at high speed. Add 1½ cups chopped, mixed candied fruits and peels. By hand, stir in 2¼ to 2¾ cups sifted all-purpose flour or enough flour to make a soft dough.

Knead on lightly floured surface till smooth and elastic, 6 to 8 minutes. Place in lightly greased bowl, turning once to grease surface. Cover; let rise in warm place till double in bulk, 1½ to 2 hours. Punch dough down. Divide dough in half; round each into a ball. Cover and let rest 10 minutes.

Pat balls of dough into 2 round loaves. Place on greased baking sheet; pat tops to flatten slightly. Cover and let rise till double, about 1½ hours. Bake at 350° about 30 minutes. (Cover tops with foil after about 25 minutes to prevent over-browning.) Cool. While still slightly warm, frost with Confectioners' Icing, and decorate with chopped nuts or nut halves and candied fruits. Makes 2 loaves.

## Sunburst Coffee Cake

>   2 packages active dry yeast
> 2¾ to 3 cups sifted all-purpose
>       flour
>   ¾ cup milk
>   ¼ cup sugar
>   ¼ cup shortening
>   1 egg
>   ½ cup raisins
>   ¼ cup candied cherries, cut up
>   2 tablespoons chopped candied
>       citron

In large mixing bowl, combine yeast and 1½ *cups* flour. Heat milk, sugar, shortening, and 1 teaspoon salt just till warm, stirring occasionally to melt butter. Add to dry mixture in bowl; add egg. Beat at low speed with electric mixer for ½ minute, scraping sides of bowl constantly. Beat 3 minutes at high speed.

Add raisins, cherries, and citron. By hand, stir in enough of the remaining flour to make a soft dough. Turn out on lightly floured surface; knead till smooth, 5 to 8 minutes. Place in a greased bowl, turning dough once. Cover and let rise till double, 1½ hours.

Punch down; turn out on a lightly floured surface. Cover and let rest 10 minutes. Divide dough into 12 equal pieces. With hands roll each piece into a rope 8 inches long and ¾ inch thick. On lightly greased baking sheet, arrange 6 pieces in a U-shape around a 4-inch circle with ends toward the center. Make the remaining 6 pieces into oval shapes and arrange over the U-shapes, with ends joining in the center. Let rise till double, about 1 hour. Bake at 350° till done, about 25 minutes. Drizzle with Confectioners' Icing and garnish with candied cherries, if desired.

## Golden Crown Coffee Bread

>   2 packages active dry yeast
>   7 tablespoons butter or margarine
>   ¾ cup sugar
>   3 eggs
>   ½ cup milk, scalded and cooled
> 3¾ cups sifted all-purpose flour
>   ¾ cup light raisins
>   2 teaspoons grated lemon peel
>   3 tablespoons fine dry bread
>       crumbs
>       Blanched whole almonds
>       Confectioners' sugar

Soften yeast in ½ cup *warm* water. In mixing bowl, cream *6 tablespoons* butter and granulated sugar until light; add eggs, one at a time, beating after each. Add softened yeast, milk, flour, and 1½ teaspoons salt. Beat at medium speed on mixer till smooth, about 2 minutes. Stir in raisins and lemon peel. Cover and let rise till double, 1½ to 2 hours.

Meanwhile, melt remaining butter. Prepare a 3-quart bundt pan or Turk's Head mold: brush liberally with melted butter and sprinkle with bread crumbs, coating well. Arrange almonds in a design on bottom of mold. Stir down batter; spoon carefully into mold. Let rise till almost double, about 1 hour. Bake at 350° till done, 25 to 30 minutes. Let stand 5 minutes; remove from mold. Cool and lightly sift confectioners' sugar over top.

**COFFEE CREAM**—Another name for 18 percent light cream. (See also *Light Cream*.)

**COFFEE GRINDER** *or* **MILL**—Equipment, hand or electrically driven, that grinds whole, roasted coffee beans. Home-sized grinders help achieve a freshly brewed coffee flavor. (See also *Coffee*.)

**COFFEE MAKER**—Any unit that is designed primarily to brew the hot beverage, coffee. (See also *Coffee*.)

**COGNAC** *(kōn' yak)*—A brandy produced around Cognac, a town in the province of Charente, in western France. The name "cognac" is protected by laws which specifically define the region and processing methods to be used when making it. No other brandies can be labeled "cognac."

Distillation of cognac began in the 1600s as a result of high taxes placed on the bulk exports of wines. The distilled wines were stronger, less bulky, brought higher prices, and provided a very palatable natural brandy superior to other liquors. Over the years, cognac has maintained this outstanding reputation.

The high quality of cognac is due to the lime soil of the district where the grapes are grown as well as to the careful distillation and aging processes the grapes undergo. St. Émilion grapes are the primary variety used, but Folle-Blanche and Colombard are also employed.

When fermentation is complete, the wine is distilled twice in traditional copperpot stills. These successive distillations produce a raw product with an alcoholic content of up to 135 proof.

The colorless liquid is then poured into barrels made of local or Limousin oak where a unique aging process takes place. No other variety of oak can produce the same characteristics. During aging, the brandy absorbs tannic acid from the barrels; this causes the color to darken and the flavor to change. Oxidation taking place in the porous wood develops the characteristic bouquet and flavor.

Because cognac is a blend, there are no vintage years. Each distiller develops his personal flavor style which he achieves, year after year, through careful blending

procedures. After several months or years of maturation, the blended brandy is bottled. Once bottled, cognac, like all distilled liquors, does not change either in color or in flavor. (See also *Brandy*.)

## Gourmet Salad

In skillet brown ½ pound chicken livers in 2 tablespoons butter or margarine. Add ½ teaspoon salt; ¼ teaspoon dried thyme leaves, crushed; and dash pepper. Remove livers.

In bowl blend ¼ cup mayonnaise or salad dressing, 1 tablespoon instant minced onion, 1 tablespoon water, and 1 tablespoon cognac (brandy). Chop livers coarsely. Add liver, ½ cup minced celery, and 2 teaspoons snipped parsley to mayonnaise mixture. Mix well; chill.

Arrange lettuce leaves on 4 chilled salad plates. Place 1 thick tomato slice on each plate; salt lightly. Spoon liver mixture onto each tomato slice. Makes 4 servings.

The colander with its functional design is ideal for tasks that involve draining foods such as vegetables and pastas.

## Cold cuts identification

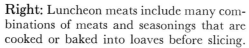

**Left:** Braunschweiger is a cooked, smoked, liver sausage that is named after the German town where it was first developed.

**Right:** Luncheon meats include many combinations of meats and seasonings that are cooked or baked into loaves before slicing.

**Left:** Cooked lamb and pork tongues are arranged lengthwise in the center of a blood sausage roll made of diced or finely ground cooked meat, beef blood, and spices.

**Right:** Peppered loaf combines coarsely ground cooked beef and pork with cracked peppercorns. The peppercorns give delightful old-fashioned flavor and texture.

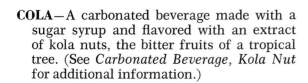

**Left:** Edible portions of pork heads are cooked, chopped, and mixed with a spiced gelatin base for headcheese. Modern formulas may include pork tongue or heart.

**Right:** Minced roll is a cooked, smoked cold cut made with finely ground beef and pork sausage. Caraway seed adds distinctive flavor to this roll—ideal for sandwiches or just plain in-between-meal nibbling.

**COLA**—A carbonated beverage made with a sugar syrup and flavored with an extract of kola nuts, the bitter fruits of a tropical tree. (See *Carbonated Beverage, Kola Nut* for additional information.)

**COLANDER** *(kul′ uhn duhr )*—A large round, perforated bowl, usually with two handles on opposite sides, made of metal or plastic. It is useful for draining liquid from foods as when rinsing noodles or spaghetti. The word "colander" is derived from a Latin word that means "to strain."

**COLCANNON** *(kuhl kan′ uhn )*—An Irish vegetable dish made by mashing potatoes, kale or other greens, and scallions. The mixture is combined with butter, milk, salt, pepper, and parsley.

**COLD CUT**—The general term for meat that is ready to eat and available fresh, canned, or packaged. Cold cuts include cooked sausages such as braunschweiger or salami, canned luncheon meats, sliced luncheon loaves, boiled ham, cured or smoked meats, and prepared meat loaves available from the delicatessen counter.

Cold cuts can be the beginning of quick-to-fix sandwiches, salads, and cold meat platters. Cold cuts and sliced cheeses, accompanied by plenty of raw vegetable relishes and an assortment of sliced dark and white breads, make a hearty self-service supper for family or buffet entertaining. Another popular use is to arrange cold cut slices or rolls around a platter, alternating them, and then to heap potato salad in the center of the platter.

## Cold cuts identification

**Left:** Olive loaf, a mild pork and beef combination, is colored and flavored with stuffed olives and sweet red peppers.

**Right:** Thuringer is a semidry summer sausage which may be either lightly or heavily smoked. It has a tangy lactic acid flavor.

**Left:** A delicate sweet flavor pervades in another versatile cold cut, honey loaf. As its name indicates, the lean pork or pork-beef mixture is seasoned with honey.

**Right:** Dry salamis are made of cured pork and beef, highly seasoned with garlic and other spices, and moistened with red wine or grape juice. The mixtures are stuffed in natural casings and air-dried.

**Left:** Jellied beef loaf has been developed for the roast beef sandwich fans. Cooked beef is shredded or chopped, mixed with gelatin, and molded into a round or rectangular loaf that is ready to slice for use.

**Right:** Pepperoni, named for its pepper spicing, is coarsely chopped meat, seasoned, cured, and then air-dried.

**Left:** Chopped ham is a popular cold cut with the hamlike flavor and color of cured pork. The ground, chopped, or cubed meat is formed into a firm loaf.

**Right:** Genoa salami (right), an Italian specialty, is identified by a light garlic flavor. Cervelatwurst (left) is a mildly seasoned summer sausage of Germany.

**Left:** Summer sausage was first made in northern Europe as a method of preserving meat for the summer. Today, it is a family name for smoked, semidry sausages.

**Right:** Frizzes, Italian dry sausages, may be purchased with sweet spices (blue string) or hot spices (red string, being sliced). Frizzes carry an abundance of flavor so slice each piece thinly for most satisfactory results.

**COLESLAW**—A salad made of shredded, crisp cabbage with well-seasoned mayonnaise or vinegar-based dressing. There are many color and flavor variations of coleslaw with added ingredients such as fruits, vegetables, and seasonings. The name is derived from the Dutch *kool* meaning cabbage and *sla* meaning salad. (See *Cabbage, Salad* for additional information.)

## Coleslaw

Shred 3 cups cabbage extra fine using chef's knife or grater. To avoid last-minute fuss toss cabbage with ice cubes; hold in refrigerator 1 hour. Remove ice; drain. If desired, add ¼ cup chopped green pepper or minced onion, *or* 1 cup grated carrots and ½ cup raisins.

Toss with one of these slaw dressings:
• Mix 2 to 3 tablespoons sugar, 3 tablespoons vinegar, 2 tablespoons salad oil, and 1 teaspoon salt; stir till sugar dissolves.
• Combine ⅓ cup mayonnaise or salad dressing, 1 tablespoon vinegar, 2 teaspoons sugar, ½ teaspoon salt, and ½ teaspoon celery seed; stir till sugar dissolves.
• In small bowl blend together ½ cup mayonnaise or salad dressing, 2 tablespoons vinegar, and 1 teaspoon prepared mustard.

## Caraway Skillet Slaw

*Cabbage in a tasty hot dressing can serve as a salad and vegetable—*

      4 slices bacon
    ¼ cup vinegar
      2 tablespoons sliced green onion
      1 tablespoon brown sugar
      1 teaspoon salt
           • • •
      4 cups shredded cabbage (about
           ½ medium head)
      1 teaspoon caraway seed

In medium skillet cook bacon till crisp. Remove bacon; drain and crumble. Measure ¼ cup bacon drippings; return to skillet. Add vinegar, onion, brown sugar, and salt; heat through. Add cabbage and caraway seed to skillet; toss mixture lightly. Top with crumbled bacon. If desired, garnish with cherry tomatoes. Serves 6.

## Spring Garden Toss

      4 cups shredded cabbage
    ½ cup chopped celery
    ¼ cup chopped green pepper
    ¼ cup shredded carrot
    ¼ cup sliced radishes
      1 tablespoon chopped onion
    ½ cup dairy sour cream
      2 tablespoons tarragon vinegar
      1 tablespoon sugar
    ½ teaspoon salt

Combine cabbage, celery, green pepper, carrot, radishes, and onion; chill. Combine remaining ingredients; chill thoroughly. Just before serving toss sour cream mixture lightly with vegetable mixture. Makes 8 servings.

## Kidney Bean Coleslaw

      3 cups shredded cabbage
      1 8-ounce can kidney beans,
           chilled and drained
    ¼ cup sweet pickle relish
    ¼ cup thinly sliced green onion
    ¼ cup mayonnaise or salad
           dressing
      3 tablespoons chili sauce
    ¼ teaspoon celery seed

Combine cabbage, kidney beans, pickle relish, and green onion; chill. Blend together mayonnaise, chili sauce, celery seed, and dash salt; toss with cabbage mixture. Makes 10 servings.

## Beet and Cabbage Slaw

    ½ 16-ounce jar pickled beets
      4 cups shredded cabbage
      2 tablespoons chopped green
           pepper
    ½ cup mayonnaise or salad
           dressing

Drain pickled beets, reserving 1½ tablespoons liquid; chop drained beets. Combine beets, shredded cabbage, and chopped green pepper; chill thoroughly. At serving time, prepare dressing by blending mayonnaise and reserved beet liquid; toss beet dressing lightly with cabbage mixture. Makes 8 servings.

Luncheon meat slices ruffle the coleslaw combination for blue cheese enthusiasts in Blue Cheese Slaw. Paprika-ladened hard-cooked egg slices create additional garnishing glamour.

### Blue Cheese Slaw

    6 cups shredded cabbage
    2 tablespoons chopped canned
        pimiento
    2 tablespoons chopped green
        onion tops
    ½ cup dairy sour cream
    2 tablespoons mayonnaise
    1 tablespoon lemon juice
    ½ teaspoon sugar
        Dash salt
    1 4-ounce package blue cheese,
        crumbled (1 cup)

Combine cabbage, pimiento, and onion tops; chill thoroughly. Mix together remaining ingredients; chill. Pour over cabbage and toss lightly. If desired, garnish bowl of coleslaw with slices of hard-cooked egg and folded luncheon meat ruffles. Makes 4 to 6 servings.

**COLLAGEN**—A protein substance of meat muscle and end-bone connective tissue.

Collagen in meats is softened by moisture and heat. The moisture may come from natural meat juices or added liquids, as when pot roast is cooked. During the cooking period, collagen is converted to gelatin, thereby producing a more tender, chewable cut of meat. (See also *Meat*.)

**COLLARD**—A dark green, leafy vegetable closely related to kale. The broad, tall collard leaves do not grow in a head as do other varieties of the cabbage family.

Because collard plants can withstand high heat and humidity, they have been grown in southern areas of the United States for generations. Traditionally, the greens are boiled with salt pork or fatback, but collard leaves can also be simmered, covered, in their own juices.

Fresh collards, when available in the grocery store, should be selected by appearance—fresh and crisp, clean and free of insect injury. Yellow or wilted leaves indicate poor quality. To retain freshness after purchase, keep crushed ice in the package of collards and refrigerate. Frozen collards are also available.

A serving of this cooked leafy vegetable is low in calories, high in vitamin A, and, if not overcooked, a good source of vitamin C. (See *Afro-American Cookery, Cabbage, Greens* for additional information.)

**COLLINS**—A tall, iced beverage of lemon or lime juice, carbonated water, and usually gin. Rum, brandy, vodka, or whiskey may be substituted for the gin.

**COLLOP**—A term sometimes used to describe a small piece or slice of meat.

**COLOR KEEPER**—A granular preparation of ascorbic acid crystals, sugar, and an inert filler designed to keep peeled or cut fruits such as apples, bananas, peaches, and pears from darkening upon exposure to air. The dry color keeper is usually diluted with water for use.

**COMB HONEY**—Honey that is sold in the beeswax comb. It is often packaged as a cut portion in a wooden box. A piece of comb honey also may be bottled with strained honey. (See also *Honey*.)

**COMBINE**—To put two or more foods together so they may be blended.

The act of combining can occur at many stages of cooking. Raisins are combined with a cooked sauce to heat them.

In salad preparation, the salad and dressing ingredients are combined separately. Before serving, they are tossed together.

When making a mix-in-one-bowl main dish, the ingredients are combined right in the baking dish—saves unnecessary washing.

**COMFIT**—A confection consisting of a solid center (such as a piece of fruit, a seed, or a nut) that is coated with sugar.

**COMICE PEAR**—An exceptionally sweet, juicy, and aromatic winter pear. The Comice pear has a fine, buttery texture and a winelike flavor. This medium- to large-sized pear has a thicker neck than most other varieties, and its pale green to yellow skin is usually blushed with red. Most sources agree that the Comice is the most delicious dessert pear grown; it is often used as the standard by which other pears are judged. Its full name is Doyenne du Comice which means "best in the show."

The Comice was originally cultivated by French and Belgian monks between 1730 and 1850 and reached America in the mid-1800s. This pear gets its name from the Comice Horticole at Angers, France, where it was extensively cultivated.

This pear is too delicate to be cooked, but it's perfect for fruit salads and fresh eating. In recent years, this pear has become increasingly favored for fruit gift boxes. The finest quality Comice pears are available between October and March.

The primary growing area for Comice pears in the United States is the Pacific Coast states of Washington, Oregon, and California. (See also *Pear.*)

**COMINO**—The Spanish name for the herb cumin. (See also *Cumin.*)

**COMPOTE**—Fresh, dried, or canned fruits gently cooked in syrup to preserve their shape. A compote may consist of one fruit or a combination of several fruits and may be served hot or cold as a dessert or main dish accompaniment. Compotes may be flavored with spices, wines, and/or liqueurs. In recent years, the definition of compote has expanded to include any fruits marinated in fruit juice or wine.

### *Delightful anytime dessert*

A dollop of sour cream crowns the luscious blend of cherries, raspberries, and strawberries in sparkling Ruby Fruit Compote.

The compote's simple ingredients and preparation invite the cook to experiment with different fruit combinations. Fruits that complement each other's color, shape, texture, and flavor can be combined for a delicious dessert that belies its simplicity. (See also *Dessert*.)

## Winter Fruit Compote

*A delicious hot dessert for winter evenings—*

> 3 firm-ripe pears, quartered and cored
> 3 baking apples, quartered and cored
> 2 oranges, peeled and chunked
> ¼ cup raisins
> ¾ cup brown sugar
> ½ cup water

Place pears, apples, oranges, and raisins in 2-quart casserole. In small bowl combine brown sugar and water; pour over fruits. Cover and bake at 350° till tender, about 1 hour. Serve warm or cool. Makes 6 servings.

## Hot Curried Fruit Compote

> 1 16-ounce can pear halves, drained
> 1 16-ounce can peach halves, drained
> 1 16-ounce can apricot halves, drained
> 1 13½-ounce can pineapple chunks, drained
> 2 tablespoons butter or margarine
> ¼ cup brown sugar
> 1 to 1½ teaspoons curry powder
> 1 17-ounce can pitted dark sweet cherries, drained

Cut pear and peach halves in half. Place pears, peaches, apricots, and pineapple chunks in a 2-quart casserole. In small saucepan melt the butter or margarine; blend in brown sugar and curry powder. Spoon over fruit in casserole. Bake at 325° for 15 minutes.

Add cherries and mix in carefully. Return to oven and bake 15 minutes more. Serve warm, as a meat accompaniment. Serves 8 to 10.

## Ruby Fruit Compote

*A great brunch starter all year round. During the winter, use frozen strawberries—*

> 1 20-ounce can frozen pitted tart red cherries, thawed
> 1 10-ounce package frozen raspberries, thawed
> 1½ tablespoons cornstarch
> 1 tablespoon lemon juice
> 1 pint whole fresh strawberries, rinsed and hulled
> Dairy sour cream

Drain frozen cherries and raspberries, reserving syrup. Add enough water to syrup to measure 2½ cups. In small saucepan blend cornstarch, dash salt, and reserved syrup. Cook and stir till thickened and clear. Add lemon juice. Stir in cherries, raspberries, and strawberries. If desired, add sugar to taste.

Chill thoroughly. Spoon into sherbets. Top each serving with a generous dollop of dairy sour cream. Makes 8 servings.

## Cherry-Berry Compote

> 1 17-ounce can pitted dark sweet cherries
> 1 10-ounce package frozen raspberries
> 2 tablespoons dry sherry

Pour undrained cherries over frozen raspberries; add sherry. Let stand about 1 hour (berries should have some ice crystals remaining). Spoon into 4 to 6 sherbets.

## Chilled Breakfast Compote

> 2 large grapefruit, peeled and sectioned
> 1 13½-ounce can frozen pineapple chunks, thawed
> ½ cup cranberry juice cocktail
> 2 or 3 dashes ground cardamom

Combine grapefruit, pineapple chunks, and their juices with cranberry juice cocktail and cardamom. Cover and chill 4 to 6 hours or overnight. Makes about 4 servings.

**CONCENTRATE**—Term applied to foods or ingredients marketed in undiluted form. This term is used most frequently in association with frozen fruit juice concentrates from which beverages can be made by the addition of water.

**CONCH** *(kongk)*—A saltwater shellfish with a spiral shell. (See also *Shellfish*.)

**CONDENSED MILK**—Sweetened fresh milk that has been thickened by evaporation of a portion of its water content. (See also *Sweetened Condensed Milk*.)

**CONDIMENT**—Anything used at the table to add flavor to food. The primary purpose of a condiment is to stimulate the taste buds and saliva secretion, thus, greatly increasing the desire for food.

Some of the principal condiments are salt, pepper, butter, vinegar, sugar, mustard, pickles, and catsup. Some foods, such as onions and garlic, are so stimulating to the taste buds and saliva secretion that they serve the double purpose of a delicious food and also a condiment.

Condiments are eaten in such small quantities that their nutritional contribution is minimal, and, except for salt, these substances are not essential to the normal functioning of the body. People, however, have become so accustomed to the flavor imparted by condiments that many foods seem bland and almost inedible without one or more of them.

**CONEY**—Name sometimes applied to a frankfurter in a long bun. A Coney Island is a coney topped with a spicy, tomato-meat sauce. (See also *Sandwich*.)

## Coney Islands

    ½ pound ground beef
    ¼ cup water
    ¼ cup chopped onion
    1 clove garlic, minced
    1 8-ounce can tomato sauce
    ½ teaspoon chili powder
    ½ teaspoon salt
    10 frankfurters
    10 frankfurter buns

For sauce, brown ground beef slowly but thoroughly in a skillet, breaking with fork till fine. Mix in water, chopped onion, minced garlic, tomato sauce, chili powder, and salt. Simmer, uncovered, for 10 minutes.

Meanwhile, cover frankfurters with cold water; bring to boiling. Simmer 5 minutes. Place franks in heated frankfurter buns; top with prepared mustard and chopped onion, if desired. Spoon hot sauce atop. Serves 10.

**CONFECTION**—A name given to a candy or sweetmeat. (See also *Candy*.)

**CONFECTIONERS' SUGAR**—A finely powdered sugar used in icing and candies. This type of sugar is often labeled XXXX. Confectioners' sugar contains about three percent cornstarch to prevent caking.

In any emergency when running slightly short of confectioners' sugar, granulated sugar, pulverized in a blender, can be used to make up the difference. This pulverized sugar is not as fine as confectioners' sugar, however, so it should not be substituted for large quantities of confectioners' sugar. (See also *Sugar*.)

## Confectioners' Icing

Add light cream to 2 cups sifted confectioners' sugar for spreading consistency. Add dash salt and 1 teaspoon vanilla.

## Caramel-Cream Cheese Frosting

    7 vanilla caramels
    1 3-ounce package cream cheese,
        softened
    2½ cups sifted confectioners'
        sugar
    ⅛ teaspoon salt

Combine caramels and 1 tablespoon hot water in a 2-cup glass measuring cup or small heat-proof glass dish. Place dish in small saucepan of gently boiling water. Heat and stir till caramels melt and sauce is smooth. Cool.

Beat together cream cheese and sugar. Add cooled caramel sauce and salt; mix well. Frosts a 1-layer cake or 18 cupcakes.

## Chocolate Crinkle Cookies

    1 cup butter or margarine
1⅓ cups sifted confectioners'
        sugar
    2 tablespoons water
    1 teaspoon vanilla
    2 4-ounce bars sweet cooking
        chocolate, grated (2 cups)
    2 cups sifted all-purpose flour
    ½ cup finely chopped walnuts

In mixing bowl cream butter or margarine and confectioners' sugar till light and fluffy. Beat in water and vanilla. Add chocolate, flour, and dash salt; mix well. Stir in nuts. Shape into 1-inch balls; place on *ungreased* baking sheet. Bake at 325° till done, about 25 minutes. Cool. Sprinkle with sifted confectioners' sugar, if desired. Makes 6 dozen.

## Saucepan Taffy Bars

    ½ cup shortening
    ⅓ cup light molasses
    ¾ cup brown sugar
    1 egg
1¼ cups sifted all-purpose flour
    ½ teaspoon salt
    ¼ teaspoon baking soda
    ⅓ cup chopped walnuts
            • • •
1½ tablespoons butter or margarine
    ⅛ teaspoon grated lemon peel
    1 to 1¼ cups sifted confectioners'
        sugar
    1 tablespoon lemon juice
    ¼ teaspoon vanilla

In saucepan heat together shortening and molasses till boiling. Remove from heat; stir in brown sugar. In mixer bowl beat egg; add molasses mixture. Beat till light and fluffy. Sift together flour, salt, and baking soda; stir into molasses mixture. Stir in nuts. Spread in greased 9x9x2-inch baking pan. Bake at 350° till done, about 20 to 25 minutes.

Frost with Lemon Butter Frosting: Cream butter or margarine with grated lemon peel. Gradually blend in ½ *cup* sifted confectioners' sugar. Beat in lemon juice and vanilla. Gradually blend in enough of remaining confectioners' sugar till of spreading consistency.

Add a touch of the tropics to toast or rolls with Peach Conserve. The double fruit conserve can also be a sundae topping.

**CONSERVE**—A jamlike spread made of several fruits cooked together with sugar. Raisins and nuts are sometimes ingredients.

## Plum Conserve

    2 pounds Italian plums
    1 cup seedless raisins
    1 medium orange
    3 cups sugar
            • • •
    ½ cup coarsely chopped walnuts

Pit plums. Grind plums, raisins, and orange (with peel). Place fruits in a large saucepan or kettle. Add sugar; bring to boiling. Cook till mixture is thick, about 10 minutes.

Stir in coarsely chopped walnuts. Pour hot conserve into hot, scalded jars. Seal at once. Makes six ½-pint jars.

## Peach Conserve

In large saucepan combine 2 pounds fully ripe peaches, scalded, peeled, and mashed (3 cups mashed), and one 6-ounce can frozen orange juice concentrate, thawed; stir in 5 cups sugar. Bring mixture to a *full rolling boil; boil hard 1 minute*, stirring constantly. Remove from heat; immediately stir in one 6-ounce bottle liquid fruit pectin and one 3½-ounce can flaked coconut. Skim off foam with metal spoon. Stir and skim for 7 minutes. Ladle into hot, scalded jars; seal. Makes seven ½-pints.

The double fruit flavor of conserve makes it different from most jams and jellies. Other fruit combinations that make delicious conserve include apples and peaches, apricots and pineapple, and rhubarb and pineapple. (See also *Jelly*.)

**CONSOMMÉ** *(kon' suh mā')* – A clear, rich soup made by boiling down meat or poultry broth until its volume is reduced by about half. The meat or poultry broth used to make consommé should not be heavily seasoned because the boiling down process intensifies the seasonings.

Further reduction of the water content of consommé will result in a product that will gel without added gelatin when chilled. Canned consommé usually contains added gelatin. (See also *Soup*.)

## Jellied Consommé

Chill canned condensed consommé (with gelatin added) in refrigerator 3 hours (or 1 hour in freezer). Spoon into chilled sherbets. Garnish with lemon and parsley. *Or*, serve in half a honeydew melon with lime slices.

For a light lunch or refreshing first course, serve Jellied Consommé, topped with sour cream, or Consommé Cooler. Accompany these chilly soups with a variety of crisp crackers.

## Consommé Cooler

        2 10½-ounce cans condensed beef
              consommé
        1 cup water
      ¼ cup finely chopped celery
        2 tablespoons finely chopped
              green onions and tops
        1 teaspoon Worcestershire sauce
              Few drops bottled hot pepper
              sauce

Combine ingredients. Chill thoroughly, at least 3 hours, stirring a few times. Float a few unpeeled cucumber slices, if desired. (To flute edges of cucumber slices, run tines of fork down cucumber.) Makes 6 to 8 servings.

## Mexican Surprises

        2 tablespoons chopped onion
        1 clove garlic, crushed
        1 tablespoon salad oil
        1 10½-ounce can condensed beef
              consommé
      ¼ cup chili sauce
        1 beaten egg
      ½ cup milk
     1½ cups soft bread crumbs
              (about 2 slices)
        1 teaspoon salt
     1½ pounds ground beef
        3 hard-cooked eggs
      ¼ cup all-purpose flour
      ⅓ cup chopped almonds (optional)

In skillet cook onion and garlic in salad oil till tender. Reserve ½ cup consommé. Add remaining consommé to skillet with chili sauce.

In mixing bowl combine beaten egg, milk, bread crumbs, and salt. Add ground beef; mix well. Cut each of the hard-cooked eggs into 6 wedges. Divide meat mixture into 18 portions. Wet hands; form one portion of meat around each egg wedge. Place meatballs in skillet with consommé mixture. Bring to boiling; reduce heat and simmer, covered, 20 minutes, turning once. Remove meatballs; reserve sauce.

Blend together all-purpose flour and reserved consommé. Stir into reserved sauce in skillet; cook and stir till thickened and bubbly. Pour over meatballs. Sprinkle with chopped almonds, if desired. Makes 6 servings.

## Lamb Roll-Ups

       12 large romaine leaves
        1 slightly beaten egg yolk
      ½ cup milk
      ⅓ cup uncooked packaged
              precooked rice
      ½ cup chopped onion
      ¾ teaspoon salt
              Dash pepper
        1 pound ground lamb
      ½ cup canned condensed beef
              consommé
        1 egg
        1 egg white
     1½ tablespoons lemon juice

Soften romaine leaves by dipping leaves in very hot water, then crushing the rib with thumb. Mix together the egg yolk, milk, uncooked rice, onion, salt, and pepper. Add ground lamb and mix thoroughly.

Shape mixture into twelve 3-inch long rolls, using about ¼ cup meat mixture for each. Place each roll lengthwise on a softened romaine leaf. Fold sides up over meat so they overlap and tuck in ends; secure with wooden picks. Place rolls in a skillet and pour consommé over. Cover; simmer 30 minutes. Pour off cooking liquid and strain; reserve for sauce.

For Lemon Sauce, beat whole egg with egg white till thick. Slowly beat in lemon juice and reserved cooking liquid. In saucepan stir over low heat till mixture thickens slightly.

Place Lamb Roll-Ups on warm serving platter. Remove wooden picks. Spoon some sauce over rolls and pass remainder. Serves 4 to 6.

**CONVENIENCE FOOD**—Food and food products that are ready for use as soon as you remove them from their package or container. (See also *Quick Cookery*.)

**CONVERTED RICE**—Rice that has been parboiled before milling. Converted rice retains more vitamins and minerals than polished rice but takes slightly longer to cook. (See also *Rice*.)

**COOKERY**—The art of preparing food. Cookery encompasses the combining, seasoning, garnishing, and serving of food that is a pleasure to eat, not just a necessity.

# COOKIE

*Easy cookies for family munching plus tasty
filled and frosted teatime delicacies.*

Cookies are small, sweet, flat, or slightly raised cakes. The name comes to us from the Dutch word *koekje*, a diminutive form of *kock* which means cake. Cookies are little cakes made from the same basic ingredients used in cakes, but formed by different methods into assorted attractive shapes. It is said that the first cookies were really tiny test cakes baked to make sure that the oven temperature and the consistency and flavor of the cake batter were just right for baking.

The first type of cookie was used by pagans in northern Europe. Small pieces of dough were imprinted with animal shapes which had been carved in wooden blocks or molds. These baked tokens were used in pagan holiday celebrations. From these crude beginnings came the beautiful molded and pressed cookies such as springerle and spritz, which are Christmas specialties from this part of the world.

Today, cookies are made in most countries, many cookies having a distinctive national character. The cookies of France are dainty and fancy. Those of Spain are thin and spicy. In the Scandinavian countries, cookies are rich, buttery, and specially shaped. Among the choicest being *krumkaker*, baked on a special iron. German cookies may be thin and dainty or large and hearty with plenty of fruits and nuts. The cookies of England, called biscuits, generally are thin, wafer tea biscuits and

## Keep the cookies coming

← Bake Mincemeat Stars, Maple Nut Chews, Cocoa Drops, Oatmeal Chip Cookies, Paul Bunyan Sugar Cookies, Caramel Chews, and Brownies. (See *Brownie* for recipe.)

are not as sweet as those from most countries. Italians also prefer cookies less sweet and frequently use anise as a flavoring.

Because the founding fathers in the New World came from so many national backgrounds, it is natural that the cookies baked by new settlers of successive generations would reflect their homelands. It wasn't long, however, before the new environment and some ingenious uses of local ingredients produced new kinds of cookies.

Early cook books and famous hostesses of the day may have insisted that cookies be made with butter, but the frontier housewife had only lard, suet, or even bear fat to use as shortening. She improvised by flavoring her cookies with spices and sweetening them with honey or molasses. Her family happily munched the results of her efforts so that keeping the cookie crock well filled was as difficult for her as it is for the modern homemaker.

Over the years America has contributed much to the international cookie jar. New England cooks provided snickerdoodles, tangle breeches, and other home-style goodies whose remarkable names were seemingly bestowed just because they were fun to repeat. More recently, brownies and sliced refrigerator cookies came into being as did cookies made with semisweet chocolate pieces. The latter were unique because the chocolate pieces stayed whole during baking. Today, the homemaker may also choose to do her baking from a wide assortment of mixes and ready-to-bake frozen or refrigerated cookies and doughs.

Cookies are favorite sweets with which to end a meal or to nibble in between meals. They come in all shapes, sizes, and flavor combinations, some with nuts and some without. Their food value is primarily to provide calories for energy. The number of calories depends upon the size of the cookie and the amount of shortening, sugar, frosting, and candies, fruits, or nuts used in making or decorating them.

Although related to cakes by virtue of common ingredients, the many kinds of cookies are as different from each other as they are from a luscious layer cake. Baking is not even a common characteristic because there are cookies which never enter an oven and some, like *fattigmand*, are cooked by frying in deep fat.

## Cookie basics

Shortening is an important ingredient in cookie baking. Butter or margarine are popular for flavor, but certain cookies are made best with a vegetable shortening, oil, or even cream cheese. Various techniques are used for incorporating the shortening. It may be creamed with the sugar, melted with chocolate, or cut into the dry ingredients with a pastry blender.

To a certain degree, the proportion of flour to liquid determines whether the final cookie will be crisp when baked or have a chewy or cakelike texture. The liquid might be milk, sour cream, fruit juice, or one of the flavorings such as vanilla, almond extract, or brandy. Of course, other factors in crispness are the thickness of the dough when it goes into the oven plus baking time and temperature.

Sweetness in cookies is a matter of personal taste. Granulated sugar, confectioners' sugar, brown sugar, honey, and molasses have been used successfully by good cooks in making cookies for centuries. The white sugars are preferred when a light color or the delicate flavor of some special ingredient is to be emphasized. The sweeteners with a dark color and distinctive flavor of their own are excellent in butterscotch bars or spicy mixtures.

The cookies themselves may be as plain or fancy as the cookie baker wishes. Bar cookies are quick to mix and bake. To serve them, simply cut in squares and transfer to a plate. Big, thick, rolled sugar cookies are just the thing for after school with a glass of milk, but the same dough rolled thinner and cut into fancy shapes, is ready to frost and decorate for a party occasion.

In addition, each homemaker has a favorite collection of cookie recipes for special occasions or for rounding out the variety of shapes and flavors offered at a tea or at an open house.

Decorating cookies is as simple as a light dusting of confectioners' sugar or as involved as ornamental frosting piped from a pastry tube. Tinted coconut, whole or chopped nuts, and candied fruits join brightly colored sugars and small candies as toppers for iced or frosted cookies.

## How to store

In many households cookies disappear almost as quickly as they are baked; thus, storage is no problem. Nevertheless, there are times when baking ahead is the order of the day and proper storage is essential to maintain the freshness of the cookies.

*In the cookie jar:* Store *soft cookies* in a container with a tight-fitting lid so that the cookies stay moist. A metal canister or a pottery jar with a snug cover are good choices. Bars and squares should be kept in the metal pan in which they were baked and covered tightly with a lid or foil. If cookies do begin to dry out, a few slices of apple or orange in the cookie jar help mellow and moisten the cookies. Remove the fruit after one or two days.

Store *crisp cookies* in a container with a loose-fitting cover. Thus, soft and crisp cookies should never be stored together. If crisp cookies do lose some of their snap, they can be freshened by heating them briefly in the oven before serving.

*In the freezer:* Most cookies, baked or unbaked, may be frozen.

Frozen dough stays fresh for up to six months. Pack the dough in a freezer container or form stiff dough into a roll and wrap securely in foil. When thawed the dough will be ready to slice and bake.

Sometimes cookie dough is formed into balls before baking. There is no reason this step can't be done before the dough goes into the freezer. Shape the balls and spread them on a baking sheet and quick-freeze an hour or until firm. Gather up the balls into a plastic bag and return to the freezer.

When it's time to bake the cookies, as many balls as desired can be baked at one time and the remainder left in the plastic bag in the freezer.

Baked cookies can be stored in the freezer for up to 12 months in plastic bags or foil. The fragile varieties are safer from possible breakage when packed in freezer containers with tight-fitting lids. When ready to serve the baked cookies, thaw them in the freezer wrappings.

*Special storage:* Students and servicemen welcome a package of home-baked goodies. The kinds of cookies as well as the packing used influence safe delivery.

---

### Cookie mailing tips

Choose soft cookies for mailing. They are better travelers than those that are crisp and breakable. Fruit-filled drops, bar cookies, or brownies pack easily and stand up well in transit. Avoid frostings and fillings that become sticky at room temperature.

A strong cardboard box or metal container is essential. Line the box with waxed paper or foil and put a cushion of crumpled newspaper, waxed paper, or plastic wrap on the bottom. Popcorn or puffed cereal should be avoided as packing materials because they sometimes attract various insects.

Wrap cookies individually or in pairs back to back using clear plastic wrap. Pack the wrapped cookies snugly in rows. Cover each layer with a cushion of crushed waxed paper or paper towels. Bar cookies baked in foil pans can be sent without removing from the pan. Be sure to allow enough space at the top of the packing box or container for a repeat of the insulation layer at the bottom.

Pack metal container, if used, into a heavy cardboard carton using crushed newspaper or confetti to hold securely. Tape box shut and tie securely. Print address on box so if wrappings come loose, address will not be destroyed. Wrap in heavy paper, address package, and label it, "Fragile, Handle with Care."

---

# Types of cookies

Most cookies are categorized according to the stiffness of the dough. The softer doughs are usually dropped by the spoonful onto a baking sheet. The stiffer ones may be chilled and sliced or rolled out on a floured board. Other doughs are pressed, molded, or baked in a sided pan. The descriptions and recipes which follow are grouped according to the final handling or shaping of the dough.

*Bar cookies:* These are cake-cookies made of a stiff dough that is spread or pressed evenly into a pan, then baked, cooled slightly, and cut into squares or diamonds. Sometimes a meringue or special topping is baked on. Usually, however, the finished bars are sprinkled with confectioners' sugar or topped with frosting.

Bar cookies generally have a thin, delicate crust and a rich, moist eating quality. A hard, crusty top is a sure sign the dough was overmixed. Overbaking should be guarded against, too, as the bars will be dry and crumbly. Fudge-type bars are done when the surface is dull in appearance and a slight imprint remains after touching the surface with a fingertip. Cakelike bars should be baked until a wooden pick inserted in the center of the pan comes out clean. Cut in bars or squares when cooled.

## Maple Nut Chews

⅓ cup butter or margarine
½ cup brown sugar
½ teaspoon maple flavoring
1 egg
½ cup sifted all-purpose flour
¼ teaspoon salt
¼ teaspoon baking powder
½ cup raisins
½ cup chopped walnuts

In a saucepan melt butter and sugar; cool slightly. Beat in maple flavoring and egg. Sift flour with salt and baking powder; stir into butter mixture. Stir in raisins and chopped walnuts; spread in a greased 8x8x2-inch pan. Bake at 350° for 25 to 30 minutes. Cool slightly before cutting into bars. Makes 16 bars.

## Cereal-Peanut Bars

*A no-bake cookie that tastes like a candy bar—*

> ½ cup light corn syrup
> ¼ cup brown sugar
> Dash salt
> 1 cup peanut butter
> 1 teaspoon vanilla
> 2 cups crisp rice cereal
> 1 cup cornflakes, slightly crushed
> 1 6-ounce package semisweet chocolate pieces (1 cup)

Combine syrup, sugar, and dash salt in saucepan; bring to a full boil. Stir in peanut butter. Remove from heat. Stir in vanilla, cereals, and chocolate pieces. Press into a buttered 9x9x2-inch pan. Chill 1 hour. Cut in small bars or squares. (For easy serving, store in refrigerator.) Makes about 2 dozen pieces.

## Candlestick Bars

*Whip up Christmas goodies quickly with mixes—*

> 1 14-ounce package gingerbread mix
> 1 8-ounce can applesauce (1 cup)
> ½ cup raisins
> ½ cup chopped mixed candied fruits and peels (4 ounces)
> 1 14-ounce package white creamy-type frosting mix
> 2 tablespoons lemon juice
> Gumdrops

Blend gingerbread mix and applesauce. Beat 2 minutes at medium speed with electric mixer or 2 minutes with spoon. Stir in raisins and fruit. Spread in greased 15½x10½x1-inch pan. Bake at 375° for 15 minutes. Substituting lemon juice for *half* the liquid, make frosting following label directions. Spread on cooled cookies. Cut in 1x1½-inch bars. Trim with candlesticks cut from gumdrops. Makes 8 dozen.

### Bonny, bonny bar cookies

← Chewy with oatmeal, buttery-rich Scotch Teas need few ingredients and only a saucepan for mixing. They're oh so easy to bake!

## Chocolate Mint Sails

Prepare one recipe of Fudge Brownies (see *Brownie* for recipe). *Or* bake 1 package brownie mix following label directions. Cool.

Combine 1 cup sifted confectioners' sugar; 2 tablespoons butter, softened; 1 tablespoon light cream; and ¼ to ½ teaspoon peppermint extract. Beat well. Tint with green food coloring. Spread over cooled brownie layer; let stand till set. Melt one 1-ounce square unsweetened chocolate with 1 tablespoon butter. Drizzle over frosting. Chill till firm. Cut in bars or triangles. Makes 2 dozen.

## Scotch Teas

Combine ½ cup butter or margarine and 1 cup brown sugar in saucepan; cook and stir till butter melts. Stir in 2 cups quick-cooking rolled oats, 1 teaspoon baking powder, and ¼ teaspoon salt. Mix well. Pour into greased 8x8x2-inch baking pan. Bake at 350° for 20 to 25 minutes. Cool; cut into bars. Makes 24 bars.

## Apple-Orange Brownies

*Mixed in a saucepan to save bowl washing—*

> 6 tablespoons butter or margarine
> 1 cup brown sugar
> ½ cup applesauce
> 1 teaspoon shredded orange peel
> 1 beaten egg
> 1 teaspoon vanilla
> 1¼ cups sifted all-purpose flour
> 1 teaspoon baking powder
> ½ teaspoon salt
> ¼ teaspoon baking soda
> ½ cup chopped walnuts
> Orange Glaze

In saucepan combine butter and brown sugar; cook and stir till melted. Beat in applesauce, orange peel, egg, and vanilla. Sift together next four ingredients; stir into mixture in saucepan. Stir in nuts. Spread in greased 15½x10½x1-inch pan. Bake at 350° for 15 minutes. While warm, top with Orange Glaze. Makes 4 dozen.

*Orange Glaze:* Combine 1½ cups sifted confectioners' sugar, ½ teaspoon vanilla, dash salt, and about 2 tablespoons orange juice.

**Drop cookies:** One of the easiest cookies to stir and bake, drop cookies get their name from the fact that the soft dough is dropped by spoonfuls onto a baking sheet. Nuts, fruits, candies, or cereals are often added to give variety in texture and flavor. Sometimes drop cookies are frosted.

Underbaking will cause a rough spot in the center of the cookies and overbaking tends to make them dry and hard with dark, crisp edges. Drop cookies are done to perfection when they are delicately browned and the imprint made by the light touch of a finger is slightly visible.

When baking a large batch of cookies, some homemakers find the cookies spread out more than desired. Chilling the dough slightly and mounding it up when dropped will help solve the problem. Making sure the cookie sheet has time to cool between batches is another good practice to follow because the heat from the pan causes the dough to melt and spread.

Meringue cookies, sometimes called kisses, are a cross between a cookie and a confection. Depending on the consistency of the mixture, they may be dropped by spoonfuls, forced through a pastry tube, or formed into balls by hand. They often have ground nuts, coconut, crushed candy, or crisp cereal folded in before baking. Although similar to the drop cookie, the macaroon is traditionally made with almond paste. Short-cut versions using sweetened condensed milk are popular, too.

## Easy Macaroons

Mix two 8-ounce packages shredded coconut, one 15-ounce can sweetened *condensed* milk (1⅓ cups), and 2 teaspoons vanilla. Drop mixture from a teaspoon onto a well-greased cookie sheet. Bake at 350° for 10 to 12 minutes. Cool macaroons slightly before removing to rack. Makes about 4 dozen macaroons.

### *A fruit cookie fantasia*

←Party favorites include Lemon Tea Cakes with coconut crowns, moist Apple-Orange Brownies, and Date-Marmalade Pastries.

## Lemon Tea Cakes

    1½ teaspoons vinegar
    ½ cup milk
    ½ cup butter or margarine
    ¾ cup granulated sugar
    1 egg
    1 teaspoon shredded lemon peel
    1¾ cups sifted all-purpose flour
    1 teaspoon baking powder
    ¼ teaspoon baking soda
    ¼ teaspoon salt
      Lemon Glaze

Stir vinegar into milk. Cream butter and sugar till fluffy. Beat in egg and peel. Sift together dry ingredients; add to creamed mixture alternately with milk, beating after each addition. Drop from teaspoon 2 inches apart on *ungreased* cookie sheet. Bake at 350° for 12 to 14 minutes. Remove at once from sheet; brush tops with Lemon Glaze. If desired, garnish with tinted coconut. Makes 4 dozen.

*Lemon Glaze:* Thoroughly blend ¾ cup granulated sugar and ¼ cup lemon juice.

## Cocoa Drop Cookies

    1 cup butter or margarine
    1¾ cups granulated sugar
    1 cup cottage cheese
    1 teaspoon vanilla
    2 eggs
    2½ cups sifted all-purpose flour
    ½ cup unsweetened cocoa
    1 teaspoon baking soda
    1 teaspoon baking powder
    ½ teaspoon salt
      Confectioners' Icing

Cream butter and sugar till fluffy. Add cottage cheese and vanilla; beat thoroughly. Add eggs, one at a time, beating well after each addition. Sift together flour, cocoa, soda, baking powder, and salt; gradually add to creamed mixture. Drop by rounded teaspoons onto greased cookie sheet. Bake at 350° about 12 minutes. Let stand briefly before removing from cookie sheet. When cool, frost with Confectioners' Sugar Icing. Makes 6½ dozen.

*Confectioners' Icing:* Combine 2 cups sifted confectioners' sugar, dash salt, and 1 teaspoon vanilla. Add milk until desired consistency.

## Oatmeal Chip Cookies

½ cup shortening
½ cup granulated sugar
½ cup brown sugar
½ teaspoon vanilla
1 egg
1 cup sifted all-purpose flour
½ teaspoon baking soda
½ teaspoon salt
1 cup quick-cooking rolled oats
1 6-ounce package semisweet
   chocolate pieces (1 cup)
½ cup chopped walnuts

Thoroughly cream shortening, sugars, and vanilla. Beat in egg, then 1 tablespoon water. Sift together flour, soda, and salt; add to creamed mixture, blending well. Stir in the rolled oats, chocolate pieces, and chopped walnuts. Drop by rounded teaspoons onto a greased cookie sheet about 2 inches apart. Bake at 375° for 10 to 12 minutes. Cool slightly before removing from pan. Makes 3½ to 4 dozen.
*Note:* For *Polka-dot Oatmeal Crisps,* substitute one 10½-ounce package candy-coated chocolate pieces for chocolate chips and nuts.

## Chocolate Yummies

1 4-ounce package chocolate
   pudding mix (regular type)
2 cups packaged biscuit mix
½ cup granulated sugar
1 slightly beaten egg
¼ cup milk
¼ cup butter or margarine,
   melted
1 teaspoon vanilla
1 3½-ounce can flaked
   coconut (1⅓ cups)
   Refrigerated ready-to-spread
   creamy chocolate frosting
   Walnut halves

Combine pudding mix (dry), biscuit mix, and sugar. Beat in egg, milk, melted butter or margarine, and vanilla. Stir in coconut. Drop dough from teaspoon onto an *ungreased* cookie sheet. Bake at 350° for 11 to 13 minutes. Remove cookies to cooling rack. Spread cooled cookies with chocolate frosting; top with walnut halves. Makes about 3 dozen cookies.

## Crunch Cookies

*Honey sweetened, spicy drop cookies—*

½ cup shortening
½ cup sugar
½ cup honey
1 egg
2 tablespoons milk
• • •
1½ cups sifted all-purpose flour
1 teaspoon salt
1 teaspoon ground cinnamon
½ teaspoon baking soda
1 cup shredded wheat cereal,
   crumbled
½ cup chopped walnuts
1 cup raisins

Cream together shortening, sugar, honey, egg, and milk. Sift together flour, salt, ground cinnamon, and baking soda; add to creamed mixture. Stir in shredded wheat cereal, nuts, and raisins. Drop from teaspoon onto greased baking sheet. Bake at 375° till lightly browned, about 12 to 13 minutes. Cool slightly before removing cookies from baking sheet. Then cool on rack. Makes about 5 dozen cookies.

*Refrigerator cookies:* The dough for these cookies is shaped into rolls, wrapped, and chilled thoroughly in the refrigerator before slicing and baking. Nuts and fruits, when used, must be finely chopped so that they do not interfere with slicing the cookies. For dainty, round cookies the dough can be shaped in a washed, empty, frozen fruit-juice container from which both ends have been removed.

Because of their high shortening content, refrigerator cookie doughs stiffen when chilled. Thus, the cold rolls of dough will slice easily with a thin, sharp knife. For best results, cut the cookies by using a back-and-forth sawing motion. Pressing down on the knife while slicing may distort the cookie's shape.

Slice and bake cookies as needed. The unbaked dough can be re-wrapped and stored in the refrigerator for up to one week or placed in the freezer for up to six months. Refrigerator cookies, baked until lightly browned, will have a crisp texture.

# Crisp Pecan Slices

*Lemony-rich cookies to slice and bake right from refrigerator or freezer—*

> ¾ cup butter or margarine
> 1 cup sugar
> 1 egg
> 1 teaspoon grated lemon peel
> 1 tablespoon lemon juice
> 2 cups sifted all-purpose flour
> 1 teaspoon baking powder
> ½ teaspoon salt
> 1 cup finely chopped pecans

Thoroughly cream butter and sugar. Add egg, lemon peel, and juice; beat well. Sift together flour, baking powder, and salt; add to creamed mixture, mixing well. Stir in finely chopped nuts. Shape in rolls 2 inches in diameter. Chill thoroughly, about 2 hours.

Using a sharp knife, slice very thin and place on *ungreased* baking sheet. Bake at 350° till delicately browned, about 10 to 12 minutes. Cool cookies slightly before removing from pan. Makes about 5 dozen cookies.

# Cherry Refrigerator Cookies

*Tender slices flavored with a dash of cinnamon—*

> 1 cup butter or margarine
> ½ cup granulated sugar
> ½ cup brown sugar
> 2 eggs
> 1 teaspoon vanilla
> 2¾ cups sifted all-purpose flour
> 1 teaspoon baking powder
> ¼ teaspoon salt
> ¼ teaspoon baking soda
>   Dash ground cinnamon
> 1 cup chopped candied cherries
> ½ cup chopped walnuts

Cream butter and sugars together till fluffy. Add eggs and vanilla; beat well. Sift dry ingredients together and stir into creamed mixture. Add cherries and nuts. Shape into rolls about 1½ inches in diameter. Wrap in waxed paper or foil and chill overnight. Slice ¼ inch thick. Place on baking sheet 1 inch apart. Bake at 375° till delicately browned, about 10 to 12 minutes. Makes 5 dozen cookies.

# Quick Sandwich Cookies

> 1 roll refrigerated slice-and-bake
>   sugar cookies
> 26 pecan halves
> ½ cup semisweet chocolate
>   pieces

Cut cookie dough into 13 slices of about ¾-inch thickness. Cut each slice into quarters. Place 2 inches apart on *ungreased* baking sheet; bake at 375° about 9 minutes. Remove from oven. Top *half* the cookie slices with a pecan half. Top each of the remaining cookies with several chocolate pieces. Return to oven for about 1 minute; remove from oven. Spread softened chocolate evenly over the chocolate-topped cookies. Place pecan-topped cookie atop each chocolate cookie. Makes 26 sandwiches.

*Rolled cookies:* These are made from a fairly soft dough which is chilled so that it is easy to handle. The dough is rolled out to the desired thickness on a lightly floured board or canvas. Cutters range from round biscuit cutters to fancy-shaped flowers, animals, or stars. Simple patterns of your own design cut from pasteboard or heavy brown paper and traced on the dough with the tip of a knife make interesting cookie shapes, too. When giant-sized cookies are wanted, a coffee can cover becomes an excellent cookie cutter.

Small amounts of chilled dough are rolled out at a time. The remainder of the dough should be returned to the refrigerator until needed. This is important because dough allowed to stand at room temperature will soften and take up more flour than necessary during rolling. Excessive re-rolling and using too much flour on the board tends to make dry, tough cookies.

Some rolled cookies are thin and crisp while others are thicker with a soft interior. Frequently, rolled cookies are folded over a filling of fruit, nuts, or frosting before baking. Sometimes the filling is spread between two baked cookies which are then put together sandwich fashion. Cookies filled before baking should be sealed well at the edges so that the filling stays inside where it belongs. Rolled and filled cookies are baked till tops are golden brown.

## Mincemeat Star Cookies

1⅓ cups shortening
1½ cups granulated sugar
2 eggs
1 teaspoon vanilla
1 teaspoon grated orange peel
4 cups sifted all-purpose flour
3 teaspoons salt
2 tablespoons milk
   Mincemeat Filling

Cream together shortening, sugar, eggs, and vanilla till light and fluffy. Stir in grated orange peel. Sift together dry ingredients; add to creamed mixture alternately with milk. Divide dough in half; chill.

On lightly floured surface, roll each half to ⅛-inch thickness. Cut cookies with 2¾-inch round cutter. Cut small star in centers of *half* the cookies. Place 1 heaping teaspoon Mincemeat Filling on each plain cookie. Top with a cutout cookie; press edges with fork to seal securely. Bake on greased baking sheet at 375° till a delicate brown, about 12 minutes. Makes 2½ dozen filled cookies.

*Mincemeat Filling:* Break one 9-ounce package mincemeat in pieces. Add 2 tablespoons granulated sugar, 2 teaspoons grated orange peel, 1 teaspoon grated lemon peel, and ¾ cup orange juice. Heat, stirring till lumps are broken; then simmer mixture about 1 minute. Cool; stir in ¼ cup chopped walnuts.

## Paul Bunyan Sugar Cookies

Cream together 1½ cups butter or margarine, 1½ cups granulated sugar, 2 eggs, and 1 tablespoon vanilla till light and fluffy. Stir in 2 tablespoons milk and ½ cup raisins. Sift together 4 cups sifted all-purpose flour, 3 teaspoons baking powder, and ½ teaspoon salt. Stir sifted dry ingredients into creamed mixture, blending well. Chill 1 hour.

On lightly floured surface, roll chilled dough to ¼-inch thickness. Cut with 2-pound coffee can or lid of round canister (about 5 inches in diameter). Sprinkle tops of cookies with granulated sugar. Place cookies about 1 inch apart on *ungreased* cookie sheet. Bake at 375° till cookies are lightly browned, about 10 minutes. Remove the baked cookies from pan with wide spatula. Makes 14 large cookies.

## Date-Marmalade Pastries

1 10-ounce package piecrust mix
1 3-ounce package cream cheese
1 tablespoon milk
1 pound pitted dates
1 cup orange marmalade

Blend piecrust mix, cream cheese, and milk. Divide dough in half. Roll each part to 10x12-inch rectangle on lightly floured surface. Cut with pastry wheel in 2-inch squares. Stuff dates with marmalade. Place date in center of each square and bring diagonal corners to center; seal. Bake at 400° till lightly browned, about 10 minutes. Makes 5 dozen.

## Creme-Filled Cookies

6 tablespoons chilled butter
1 cup sifted all-purpose flour
2½ tablespoons light cream
¾ cup sifted confectioners' sugar
1 tablespoon butter, softened
⅛ teaspoon almond extract
1 tablespoon light cream

With pastry blender or fork, cut the 6 tablespoons butter into flour till size of small peas. Sprinkle *1 tablespoon* cream over part of mixture. Gently toss with fork; push to one side of bowl. Sprinkle *next tablespoon* cream over dry part; mix lightly. Push to moistened part at side. Repeat with remaining ½ tablespoon of cream till all is moistened. Carefully gather dough up with fingers; form in ball.

For easier handling, divide dough in half. On lightly floured surface, roll to slightly less than ⅛ inch. Cut dough in 1½-inch squares with pastry wheel. Dip one side of each cookie in sugar. Place sugar side up, ½ inch apart, on *ungreased* cookie sheet. With fork prick each cookie in parallel rows.

Bake at 375° till golden brown and puffy, about 8 minutes. Remove at once to cooling rack. When cookies are cool, sandwich with Almond Filling. Garnish with a dollop of Confectioners' Icing, if desired, and a few pieces of sliced toasted almonds. Makes 2½ dozen.

*Almond Filling:* Thoroughly combine confectioners' sugar, the 1 tablespoon butter, almond extract, and the 1 tablespoon light cream (or enough for spreading consistency).

Twin tiers show off Caramel Chews, Browned Butter Nuggets, Quick Sandwich Cookies, Candlestick Bars, Chocolate Yummies, and Coconut Cake Bars. (See *Coconut* for bars recipe.)

***Shaped and pressed cookies:*** Since both of these cookies require special handling, they are considered here together. The dough is pliable and may need to be chilled if it becomes too soft to work with.

Shaped cookies are formed by hand. Small pieces of dough are rolled into a smooth ball or pencil-shaped roll with the palms of the hands. Sometimes the dough is wrapped around pieces of date, candied fruit, or nutmeats. When baked, some cookies keep their prebaked form, while others flatten slightly or crinkle on top. In many recipes the balls are flattened before baking with the bottom of a glass which has been dipped in granulated sugar or flour. Crisscross marks made with the tines of a fork make a pretty pattern, too. Or, a thumbprint in the soft dough leaves an indentation just the right size to fill with colorful jam or jelly after baking.

The dough for pressed cookies is forced through a cookie press into desired shapes and designs. Spritz are perhaps the best known of the dainty pressed cookies. The necessary equipment for making stars, Christmas trees, and assorted shapes comes with the cookie press. The manufacturer's directions should be followed when using a press. (See also *Christmas*.)

## Jam Thumbprints

  ⅔ cup butter or margarine
  ⅓ cup granulated sugar
  2 egg yolks
  1 teaspoon vanilla
  ½ teaspoon salt
  1½ cups sifted all-purpose flour
  2 slightly beaten egg whites
  ¾ cup finely chopped walnuts
    Strawberry preserves or currant
      jelly

Cream together butter and sugar until fluffy. Add egg yolks, vanilla, and salt; beat well. Gradually add sifted flour, mixing well.

Shape dough into ¾-inch balls; dip in slightly beaten egg whites. Roll in chopped walnuts. Place 1 inch apart on greased cookie sheet. Press down center of each with thumb.

Bake cookies at 350° till done, about 15 to 17 minutes. Cool slightly; remove from cookie sheet and cool on rack. Just before serving fill centers of cookies with preserves or jelly. Makes about 3 dozen cookies.

## Browned Butter Nuggets

  1 2⅞-ounce package whole, shelled
    filberts (about 2½ dozen)
  ½ cup butter or margarine
  ¼ cup sifted confectioners' sugar
  ½ teaspoon vanilla
  1½ cups sifted all-purpose flour

Toast filberts in 325° oven for 10 minutes. Brown butter in saucepan. Remove from heat; immediately blend in confectioners' sugar and vanilla. Cool. Blend in flour. Shape a rounded teaspoon of dough around each nut to form balls. Place on *ungreased* cookie sheet.

Bake at 325° for 20 minutes. Cool slightly on cookie sheet; remove. When cool, sift additional confectioners' sugar over cookies, if desired. Makes about 2½ dozen nuggets.

### *Welcome world travelers*

←Salute friends with a slide-viewing party. Parade Creme-Filled Cookies, jam-topped Tasty Pastries, and Chocolate Mint Sails.

## Frosty Date Balls

  ½ cup soft butter or margarine
  ⅓ cup sifted confectioners' sugar
  1 tablespoon water
  1 teaspoon vanilla
  1¼ cups sifted all-purpose flour
    Dash salt
  ⅔ cup chopped pitted dates
  ½ cup chopped walnuts

Cream together butter and sugar. Stir in water and vanilla. Add flour and salt. Mix well. Stir in dates and walnuts. Roll in 1-inch balls. Place 2½ inches apart on *ungreased* cookie sheet. Bake at 300° till cookies are set but not brown, about 20 minutes. While warm, roll in confectioners' sugar. Makes about 2½ dozen.

## Caramel Chews

Place 36 vanilla caramels (10 ounces) and 3 tablespoons light cream in top of a double boiler over simmering water. Heat till caramels melt; stir occasionally. Toss together 1 cup cornflakes, 2 cups crisp rice cereal, 1 cup flaked coconut, ½ cup chopped walnuts, and ½ cup raisins. Pour caramel mixture over. Mix thoroughly. With buttered fingers, press rounded tablespoons of mixture lightly into balls. Place on waxed paper. Makes 4 dozen.

## Tasty Pastries

  1 package active dry yeast
  ¼ cup *warm* water
  1 10-ounce package piecrust mix
  1 tablespoon granulated sugar
  1 egg yolk
  ½ cup strawberry preserves, orange
    marmalade, *or* boysenberry jam

Soften yeast in warm water. Blend piecrust mix, sugar, egg yolk, and the softened yeast; mix well. Roll dough into balls the size of a small walnut. Place on *ungreased* cookie sheet. Make deep indentation in center of each ball, shaping into shells 1½ inches in diameter and ¼ inch deep. Spoon one teaspoon of jam into each shell. Let rise in warm place 1 hour.

Bake at 375° for 12 to 15 minutes. Cool slightly; remove from sheet. Makes 3 dozen.

Christmas tree, star, and Santa Claus cookies have developed into traditional holiday treats made with cookie cutters.

The cookie press eliminates the rolling step and is capable of producing a large variety of tasty, shaped cookies.

Turning the handle at the top forces dough through the desired opening. The disks can easily be switched to change the design.

**COOKIE CUTTER**—A utensil for cutting rolled dough into shaped cookies. Cookie cutters are similar to biscuit cutters but are usually a fancier shape.

**COOKIE PRESS**—A useful utensil for forming soft dough into different cookie shapes. A hollow tube holds the dough while a plunger forces the dough through a shaped opening. The design of the opening can be varied by interchanging metal disks.

**COOKIE SHEET**—A flat, broad metal sheet on which rolls, biscuits, cookies, and cream puffs may be baked. The thin metal from which cookie sheets are constructed, usually aluminum or tin, allows heat to be transmitted rapidly to the food being baked. Shiny sheets allow for more even browning than when the luster is lost.

When selecting cookie sheets, look for at least one turned-up edge for easy grasping and an open edge for easy removal.

**COOKING WINE**—A low-quality wine sold in grocery stores, often seasoned with salt making it unfit for drinking.

When wine is used in cooking, the alcohol is driven off by the cooking heat; only the wine flavor remains. For this reason,

*A summer cooler*

The irresistible beverage Raspberry Mint→ Cooler combines lemonade, raspberries, and fresh mint. (See recipe on page 616.)

many cooks prefer to utilize one of the less expensive table wines rather than cooking wine. If only a little wine is needed, use some of the same wine that is to be served with the meal for the desired cooking purpose. (See also *Wines and Spirits*.)

**COOL**—To remove food from heat and to let it stand at room temperature. Many recipes specify cooling prior to adding ingredients which cannot tolerate heat.

**COOLER**—A tall, refreshing fruit or milk drink usually served with ice. Coolers are especially thirst-quenching on a hot day.

## Raspberry Mint Cooler

*Pictured on page 615—*

½ cup lightly packed fresh mint
    leaves
¼ cup sugar
1 cup boiling water
. . .
1 10-ounce package frozen red
    raspberries
1 6-ounce can frozen lemonade
    concentrate
2 cups cold water

Combine sugar, mint leaves, and boiling water; let stand 5 minutes. Add raspberries and lemonade concentrate; stir till thawed. Add cold water and stir. Serve over ice. Makes 8 servings.

## Sparkling Mint Cooler

1 10-ounce jar mint jelly
    (about 1 cup)
2 12-ounce cans unsweetened
    pineapple juice (3 cups)
½ cup lemon juice
1 28-ounce bottle ginger ale,
    chilled (3½ cups)

Combine jelly and 1½ cups water. Heat and stir over low heat till jelly melts; cool. Add pineapple and lemon juices; chill. To serve, place ice cubes in tall glasses; fill *half* full with fruit mixture. Fill remaining half with ginger ale. Stir to blend. Serves 10.

**COOLIE PAN**—Another name for the Chinese utensil, the wok. (See also *Wok*.)

**COOLING RACK**—A wire rack elevated to permit complete air circulation and used for cooling baked products such as cakes.

**COON CHEESE**—A sharp, aged Cheddar cheese with a dark rind. The interior of coon cheese is yellow in color, crumbly in texture, and sharp in flavor.

The patented method for preparing coon cheese involves higher temperatures and humidity than for other Cheddar cheeses. (See also *Cheddar Cheese*.)

**COPPER**—A pinkish brown metal used in kitchen utensils. Copper has been in abundant domestic use for hundreds of years. Formerly, cooking utensils were wholly copper; today, its properties are used to best advantage when copper is combined with or applied over other metals.

The most advantageous property of copper is its ability to spread heat evenly and quickly. In this respect, it is the cooking world's best heat conductor. Copper is also very ductile and malleable. For utensils, it may be drawn into very fine wire, hammered into thin sheets, and rolled, stamped, or pressed.

*How copper utensils are produced:* Copper is rarely used alone for household utensils. When applied to the bottom or as an inner layer of the bottom of a saucepan or skillet, the utensils' heating properties are improved vastly. In most instances, copper is electroplated onto stainless steel, a poor heat conductor. Whether a bottom layer or a core, the copper usually extends a short way up the sides of the pan so that the heat spreads evenly for uniform cooking.

*How to use:* The major disadvantage of using copper cookware is its tendency to tarnish on exposure to heat. Manufacturers coat some copper-bottomed utensils with a lacquer that prevents darkening. This finish, however, is not permanent and is unsightly while wearing off the pan.

Frequent cleaning of copper pans is needed to maintain attractive appearance. Dipping the copper portion in vinegar, then rubbing with salt, or using one of various copper cleaners, satisfactorily removes the thin film of copper oxide. (See *Pots and Pans, Saucepan,* and *Utensil* for additional information.)

**COQ AU VIN** *(kôk ô van')* — A popular French chicken dish made with red wine (frequently red Burgundy) and usually cooked with onions, mushrooms, bacon or salt pork, herbs, and seasonings.

## Coq au Vin

*Typical accompaniments to serve include parslied potatoes and buttered green peas—*

      4 slices bacon, cut in small
          pieces
      2 tablespoons chopped onion
      1 2½- to 3-pound ready-to-
          cook broiler-fryer chicken,
          cut up
      •   •   •
      8 shallots *or* small whole onions
      ½ cup coarsely chopped carrots
      1 clove garlic, minced
      2 tablespoons brandy (cognac)
      •   •   •
      1 pint fresh mushrooms, sliced
      2 tablespoons butter
      3 to 4 sprigs parsley
      1 medium whole bay leaf
      ¼ teaspoon dried thyme leaves,
          crushed
      1 celery stalk with leaves, cut up
      2 cups red Burgundy

In skillet brown bacon pieces and chopped onion; remove from skillet. Add chicken pieces and brown slowly in bacon drippings; remove chicken. Add shallots, carrot, garlic, and brandy; cook mixture about 3 minutes. Meanwhile, cook mushrooms with butter in skillet.

Make *Bouquet Garni:* In a tea ball or cheese-cloth bag combine parsley, bay leaf, thyme, and celery; tie cheesecloth bag securely. Place in a 2-quart casserole. Layer chicken, vegetables, and mushrooms in casserole.

Add wine to the skillet; heat to boiling and stir to loosen the crusty brown bits. Pour mixture over casserole. Cover; bake at 350° for 2 hours. Remove Bouquet Garni. Serves 4.

**COQUILLE** *(kō kil')* — An authentic or artificial scallop shell used for baking and attractively serving any number of seafood and creamed mixtures.

**COQUILLE ST. JACQUES** *(-san zhäk)* — 1. A French term for scallops. 2. The recipe name for scallops cooked in a rich, creamy wine sauce and baked in a coquille. Mushrooms and other shellfish are sometimes added to the scallop mixture.

The recipe title "Coquille St. Jacques" has an interesting origin. Pilgrims and crusaders who visited the Spanish shrine, St. James of Compostella, ate the scallop dish as penance instead of eating meat. The empty coquilles were then fastened to the pilgrims' hats for the journey home.

Small whole onions and sliced fresh mushrooms top well-sauced Coq au Vin, a French creation for the food connoisseur.

**CORAL**—The roe of female lobsters. During cooking, the roe turn coral red. This edible portion of lobster has a delicious flavor. Coral is also used to color sauces or lobster butter. (See also *Lobster*.)

**CORDIAL** *(kôr′ juhl)*—A name for an alcoholic after-dinner drink or liqueur. The word "cordial" is derived from the Latin word *cordialis* meaning "of or belonging to the heart." In England, it also refers to a sweet, water-mixed drink.

**CORDON BLEU** *(kôr dôn blœ′)*—1. The French term for blue ribbon and name of the most renowned classic French cooking school. The institution, established in Paris in 1700, was initially a girls' school until the fame of its cooking program resulted in a change in curriculum. 2. Sauced meat rolls of veal, ham, and cheese.

**CORIANDER**—A lacy-looking plant of the parsley family native to the Mediterranean region. The coriander plant has been nicknamed Chinese Parsley.

The flavor extracted from coriander leaves and seeds has been regarded highly throughout the centuries. Long ago, Asians used coriander in curry mixtures. Archaeological investigations have unearthed coriander seeds from Egyptian tombs. Ancient writings of Babylon refer to coriander's fragrance in the Hanging Gardens, and the Hebrews described their manna as "like coriander seed, white." In Roman and Grecian cooking, too, coriander was a very popular seasoning.

Difficulty in harvesting the crop accounts for importation rather than regional production of coriander in the United States. For successful harvesting, the seeds must be completely ripe to taste good; but at this stage of development, seeds fall to the ground at the slightest touch. Consequently, even though the coriander plant would grow easily here, production would not be economical. Therefore, the seeds are imported from Morocco, Romania, Argentina, and France.

Nationalities in Latin America, Russia, and Eastern Europe use coriander leaves in cooking. The Spanish call the leaves *cilantro*. In the United States, however, the dried fruits or seeds, white to yellow brown in color, are the only form normally available. The whole, round seeds are tiny, measuring about one-eighth inch in diameter. They may be purchased in two forms, either whole or ground.

Coriander seed has numerous commercial and household uses. It is the traditional "heart" of old-fashioned candies called comfits. The ever-popular frankfurter and sausage would be at a loss without the flavor of coriander. In addition, it is one of the major ingredients in curry powder and mixed pickling spices, and it is a flavoring agent used in gin. Coriander is also used to give scents to some perfumes.

The delightful aroma and taste—somewhat like lemon and sage—adds appealing flavor to cookies, candies, Danish pastry, and gingerbread as well as to beef or pork roasts, game, cheeses, and soups. (See *Herb, Spice* for additional information.)

## Spareribs Far East

*An exotic sauce for spareribs—*

   3 pounds pork spareribs
  ¼ cup salad oil
  ¼ cup soy sauce
  2 tablespoons lemon juice
  1 tablespoon instant minced onion
  1 tablespoon coriander seed, crushed
  1 tablespoon brown sugar
  ¾ teaspoon hickory smoke–flavored salt
  ½ teaspoon ground cumin
  ½ teaspoon ground ginger
  ¼ teaspoon pepper

If desired, cut spareribs into serving-size pieces. Place on rack in shallow baking pan. Bake at 450° for 30 minutes; drain off fat from pan. Reduce oven temperature to 350° and bake the spareribs 30 minutes longer.

Combine salad oil, soy sauce, lemon juice, onion, crushed coriander, brown sugar, smoke-flavored salt, cumin, ginger, and pepper. Spoon or brush sauce over ribs on all sides. Continue baking till ribs are tender, about 1 hour, continuing to baste them occasionally with the barbecue sauce. Makes 4 servings.

## Coriander Cookies

      1 cup butter or margarine
      1 cup sugar
      2 eggs
   2¾ cups sifted all-purpose flour
      4 teaspoons ground coriander
      1 teaspoon baking soda
   ½ teaspoon cream of tartar
         Dash salt
      2 tablespoons water
         Sugar

Cream together butter and the 1 cup sugar; add eggs and beat till fluffy. Sift together flour, coriander, baking soda, cream of tartar, and salt; blend into creamed mixture. Add water; beat well. Drop from teaspoon onto *ungreased* cookie sheet. Flatten with the bottom of a glass dipped in sugar. Bake at 375° for 8 to 10 minutes. Cool on rack. Makes 5 dozen.

**CORKSCREW**—A piece of equipment for removing corks from bottles. Many variations of the traditional corkscrew have been developed, but most of them work on similar principles. A sharp-pointed metal spiral is attached at right angles to the handle. The metal spiral should be thin, tapered, and sharp at the point only. If the edges are sharp, they will make the cork crumble. The spiral is inserted into the cork with a twisting motion. Removal of the cork may be facilitated by means of levers on the corkscrew.

A modern variation of the corkscrew is an instrument that injects a small amount of harmless gas through the cork into the bottle. The gas forces the cork out.

**CORKY**—A term for wines that have off-flavors due to defective corks. These wines are not recommended for drinking.

Spareribs Far East boasts a distinctive oriental flavor. Included in the seasoning blend is coriander seed, an aromatic member of the parsley family that tastes somewhat like a blend of lemon and sage. Shown in the mortar and pestle are whole coriander seeds.

**CORN**—A seed or kernel of the cereal plants that is used for food. In many countries, corn refers to the main crop: in England, it refers to wheat; in Scotland and Ireland, to rye. However, in America, corn refers to Indian corn or maize. Individual ears of the maize type of corn consist of kernels growing on cobs which are surrounded by fine silks and an outside husk.

The confusion in definition is carried through in the multitude of uses to which corn has been put. For instance, the Indians of Central America, Peru, and Mexico used corn as a food, as a fuel, as a building material, as jewelry, and also as a form of money for buying other items.

Although we must speculate as to corn's place of origin, archaeological findings point to Mexico or Central America. Wild corn did exist in Mexico prior to 3,000 B.C. Most probably, present-day varieties are descendents of this early wild corn. Unlike many other seeds, American corn is not wind-borne and does not seed itself. It has to be carried by hand and planted. It is not known exactly how corn was carried from Central America to North America, but it is known that in the late fifteenth century Columbus introduced corn kernels to the Spanish people.

In America, corn is most closely associated with American Indians who taught the early European settlers how to grow, harvest, and use corn. The Indians also taught settlers how to cook many Indian dishes. Some of these have become traditional American recipes. For example, succotash, a cooked corn and bean combination, is a recipe of the Indians.

Corn has undergone many changes throughout the years. From its former multicolored (red, white, yellow, and black) appearance, corn has been changed by hybridization to a single color variety, adaptable to a wide range of climates.

*Nutritional value:* Corn contributes carbohydrates to the diet, one medium ear adding about 95 calories. One-half cup canned whole kernel corn equals about 70 calories; cream-style corn adds a few more calories. Corn also contains some vitamin C, B vitamins, thiamine, and riboflavin, plus some vitamin A in the yellow varieties.

*Types of corn:* There are several types of corn, including field (dent), flint, flour, pop-, sweet, waxy, and pod. However, only a few are important to the homemaker.

Up until the mid-nineteenth century, field corn was the most common variety found on the dinner table. But with great strides in the cultivation of corn hybrids, sweet corn was developed and has become the most popular variety for eating.

Field corn, also called dent corn, is used mainly in the manufacture of cereals, starches, and other corn products. It is used also as animal feed. Much of the livestock and poultry in America is corn-fed.

The other major type is sweet corn, also called corn-on-the-cob. This type of corn has a high sugar content, thus, making it very good to eat. The sweet corn kernels are more tender and the ears are slightly smaller than those of field corn.

There are also other varieties of corn grown on a limited scale. They are used in the manufacturing of food and other products. These include popcorn and the tiny sweet corn ears that are used for pickling.

*How to select:* Sweet corn can be purchased fresh almost all year round in some areas, but the peak time for this crop is during the summer months. Because it's perishable, purchase just before using.

Choose ears that are well filled with even rows of plump, milky kernels. To find out if the kernels are milky, apply slight pressure on them. The kernels should puncture. Tiny kernels on the cob most often are immature and will lack flavor. The husk should have a fresh, green color, and the ears should be without worm damage.

Corn, either whole kernel or cream-style, is also available canned. It can be purchased frozen—on the cob, cut off the cob, or mixed with other vegetables. Pickled miniature corn-on-the-cob can be purchased in many gourmet food shops.

### All-American corn on the cob

For best eating, choose sweet corn that has → plump, milky kernels. Pass fluffy seasoned butters with the hot cooked corn.

*How to store:* Use fresh corn as soon as possible after purchasing for best eating quality. Because the sugars in the kernel start turning to starch after it is picked, corn will lose its sweet flavor quickly, especially if stored unrefrigerated. Store it in the coolest part of the refrigerator as soon as possible after picking. If desired, the husks can be removed from the ears, then the ears can be placed in a plastic bag or wrapped in foil and refrigerated.

For out-of-season use, corn can be canned by either hot-pack or raw-pack methods, as whole kernel or cream-style corn. For whole kernel corn, the cob is not scraped. Cream-style corn is prepared by cutting only about half the kernel off the cob, then scraping the cob.

Or, corn can be frozen either on the cob or cut off. To freeze corn-on-the-cob, husk and remove silks. Wash and sort. Don't use overmature corn. Blanch small ears 7 minutes in boiling water, medium ears 9 minutes, and large ears 11 minutes. Chill in cold water, changing water frequently, allowing about the same amount of time for cooling as for blanching. To freeze the kernels, blanch corn 4 minutes, cool, then cut corn off cob. Store in moisture-vaporproof containers in the freezer.

---

*Ways to prepare fresh corn*

Corn on the cob: Remove husks, then silks with a stiff brush. Rinse and cook, covered, in small amount of boiling salted water (or cook in enough boiling salted water to cover) about 6 to 8 minutes. Don't overcook.

Foil-baked corn: Spread butter on husked corn, then sprinkle with salt and pepper. Wrap in foil. Bake at 450° about 25 minutes. Turn several times during baking. Or, cook wrapped corn (don't seal seam) on grill over *hot* coals 15 to 20 minutes, turning often.

Cut corn: Cut off just the tips from kernels with a sharp knife and scrape cobs with dull edge of knife. Cook, covered, in small amount of boiling salted water, or in milk, or butter till corn is done, 5 to 8 minutes.

---

*How to use:* The list of uses for corn is long. Consequently, there is a corn dish to suit every occasion, from a backyard barbecue corn-on-the-cob to fancy corn presented in a silver serving dish. An assortment of corn recipes would include soups and chowders, both main dish and vegetable casseroles, skillet dishes, quick breads, puddings, scallops, and relishes.

When eating corn-on-the-cob, use plastic handles and insert them in the ends of the ears of corn. Serve with plenty of butter, either plain or whipped, and pass snipped chives, salt, and pepper so each person can season to his individual taste.

## Deviled Corn and Crab

¼ cup butter or margarine
2 tablespoons all-purpose flour
1 tablespoon lemon juice
1 teaspoon prepared mustard
½ teaspoon salt
½ teaspoon Worcestershire sauce
  Dash pepper
½ cup milk
1 7½-ounce can crab meat, drained, flaked, and cartilage removed
2 hard-cooked eggs, chopped
1 17-ounce can whole kernel corn, drained
1 17-ounce can cream-style corn

• • •

½ cup grated Parmesan cheese
½ cup medium saltine cracker crumbs (about 14 crackers)
1 tablespoon butter, melted
  Hard-cooked egg
  Pimiento-stuffed green olives

In saucepan melt the ¼ cup butter; stir in flour, lemon juice, mustard, salt, Worcestershire sauce, and pepper. Add milk all at once; cook and stir till mixture thickens and bubbles. Remove from heat; carefully stir in crab meat, chopped hard-cooked eggs, whole kernel corn, and cream-style corn.

Spoon into a 1½-quart casserole; sprinkle cheese over top. Combine cracker crumbs and the 1 tablespoon melted butter; sprinkle over cheese. Bake at 350° till heated through, about 45 minutes. Garnish with hard-cooked egg wedges and olive slices. Makes 6 servings.

Two kinds of corn—whole kernel and cream-style—are included in the ingredient list for Deviled Corn and Crab. To make it a main dish casserole, pieces of crab are also incorporated.

## Mexican-Style Hash

*Yesterday's roast beef gets a flavor boost with the addition of corn and tomato soup—*

In oven-going skillet cook 2 cups coarsely ground or diced cooked roast beef and ⅓ cup chopped onion in 2 tablespoons shortening till onion is tender but not brown. Add 1½ cups finely chopped, peeled raw potatoes; one 12-ounce can whole kernel corn, drained; one 10¾-ounce can condensed tomato soup; and ¼ teaspoon chili powder. Stir till thoroughly mixed. Cover skillet with foil. Bake at 350° for 35 to 40 minutes. Makes 4 servings.

## Indian Corn Casserole

*Bacon adds special flavor—*

In a bowl combine 3 well-beaten eggs, ¼ cup all-purpose flour, and 2 tablespoons sugar. Beat mixture thoroughly. Add 6 ounces sharp process American cheese, shredded (1½ cups), and two 17-ounce cans whole kernel corn, drained. Cook 10 slices bacon till crisp. Drain and crumble. Stir in ¾ *of the bacon.*

Turn mixture into a 10x6x1½-inch baking dish. Sprinkle remaining bacon atop. Bake at 350° till knife inserted in center comes out clean, about 30 minutes. Makes 8 servings.

## Ham Succotash

    2 9-ounce packages frozen cut
        green beans
    2 17-ounce cans whole kernel corn,
        drained
    2 17-ounce cans cream-style corn
    2 cups soft bread crumbs (about
        3 slices bread)
    2 beaten eggs
    1 tablespoon instant minced onion
    2 teaspoons dry mustard
    2 teaspoons dried basil leaves,
        crushed
    1 teaspoon salt
    ½ pound boneless fully cooked ham
        sliced ½ inch thick
    1 6-ounce can sliced mushrooms,
        drained
    1 pound boneless fully cooked ham,
        cut into serving pieces

Add frozen beans to boiling salted water. Return just to boiling; drain. Set aside.

Combine whole kernel corn, cream-style corn, bread crumbs, eggs, instant onion, dry mustard, basil, salt, and dash pepper.

Cut the ½ pound of ham into cubes. Stir into corn mixture with drained beans and mushrooms. Turn into 3-quart casserole. Bake, uncovered, at 350° for 1 hour. Arrange ham pieces atop corn mixture. Bake, uncovered, 30 minutes longer. Makes 12 servings.

## Beef and Vegetable Skillet

    2 pounds ground beef
    1 15-ounce can tomato sauce
    1 12-ounce can whole kernel corn,
        undrained
    1 10-ounce package frozen okra,
        thawed, and cut into ¾-inch
        pieces
    1 tablespoon brown sugar
    4 slices sharp process American
        cheese

In skillet brown meat; drain. Sprinkle with ½ teaspoon salt. Add tomato sauce, undrained corn, okra, and brown sugar. Bring to boiling; reduce heat. Cover; simmer 10 minutes. Arrange cheese slices atop. Cover; heat 3 to 4 minutes to melt cheese. Makes 8 servings.

## Corn Pancakes with Chili

    1 pound ground beef
    1 tablespoon butter or margarine
    ½ envelope dry onion soup mix
    2 teaspoons chili powder
    ¼ teaspoon garlic powder
    1 16-ounce can red kidney beans
    2 8-ounce cans tomato sauce

        • • •

    3 eggs
    1 cup sifted all-purpose flour
    1 tablespoon sugar
    1 tablespoon baking powder
    1¼ cups buttermilk
    2 tablespoons butter, melted
    3 tablespoons yellow cornmeal
    ½ cup whole kernel corn, drained
    ¾ cup shredded Cheddar cheese

Brown meat in 1 tablespoon butter. Stir in soup mix, chili powder, garlic powder, beans with liquid, and tomato sauce. Simmer, uncovered, 30 minutes; keep warm.

Beat eggs till light and fluffy. Sift together next 3 ingredients and ½ teaspoon salt; add to eggs. Beat till almost smooth. Stir in buttermilk and 2 tablespoons melted butter; beat just till smooth. Stir in cornmeal and corn. Bake on hot, lightly greased griddle till golden brown, using ¼ cup batter for each. To assemble, spoon ⅓ cup meat on each pancake; fold. Top each with 1 tablespoon shredded cheese. Serve hot. Makes 10 to 12 five-inch pancakes.

## Corn Pancakes

Sift together 1 cup sifted all-purpose flour, 2 teaspoons baking powder, and ½ teaspoon salt. Blend 2 well-beaten eggs; ¾ cup light cream; one 17-ounce can cream-style corn; and ¼ cup butter or margarine, melted. Add to flour mixture and stir just till moistened.

Fry in greased skillet using ¼ cup batter for each pancake. Turn when top is bubbly and a few bubbles have broken. Add extra shortening as needed to fry pancakes. Makes 16 pancakes.

To serve, top with *Hard Sauce:* Cream ½ cup butter or margarine and 2 cups sifted confectioners' sugar till fluffy. Beat in 1 egg, 2 tablespoons brandy, and ¼ teaspoon vanilla. Chill. Spoon on pancakes and sprinkle with ground nutmeg. Makes 1⅓ cups sauce.

## Speedy Corn Fritters

1 cup buttermilk pancake mix
½ teaspoon baking powder
1 8¾-ounce can whole kernel
   corn, drained
1 6-ounce can evaporated milk
   Fat for frying

Combine pancake mix and baking powder. Add drained corn and evaporated milk. Stir just till blended. Drop from tablespoon into deep hot fat (375°). Fry until golden brown, about 2 minutes. Drain on paper toweling. Serve with butter, if desired. Makes about 32.

## Corn Fritters

Cut off tips of kernels from 3 to 4 ears fresh corn, then scrape cobs to make 1 cup cut corn with liquid. (*Or* use one 8¾-ounce can whole kernel corn.) Drain corn, reserving liquid. Add enough milk to liquid to measure 1 cup.

Sift together 1½ cups sifted all-purpose flour, 3 teaspoons baking powder, and ¾ teaspoon salt. Combine 1 beaten egg, milk mixture, and corn. Add to dry ingredients. Mix just till moistened. Drop batter from tablespoon into deep hot fat (375°). Fry until golden brown, 3 to 4 minutes. Drain fritters on paper toweling. Serve with warm maple syrup, if desired. Makes 2 dozen fritters.

## New England Corn Chowder

4 slices bacon
1 medium onion, thinly sliced
2 cups diced, peeled, raw potatoes
1 17-ounce can cream-style corn
2 cups light cream
1 tablespoon butter or margarine

In saucepan cook bacon till some of fat is fried out. Add onion; cook till bacon is crisp and onion lightly browned. Remove bacon; drain on paper toweling. (Drain off excess fat from saucepan.) To saucepan add 2 cups water, potatoes, and salt and pepper to taste; cover and simmer 20 minutes. Add corn and cream; simmer 5 minutes longer. Crumble the bacon; just before serving, add bacon bits and butter to corn mixture. Makes 6 to 8 servings.

## Beef–Corn Chowder

1 10½-ounce can condensed beef
   noodle soup
¼ cup chopped green pepper
2 tablespoons chopped onion
1 17-ounce can whole kernel corn
½ cup cooked, diced, peeled
   potatoes
2 cups milk
   Dash white pepper

In a saucepan combine condensed soup, green pepper, and onion. Simmer, covered, till vegetables are tender. Add corn plus liquid, potatoes, milk, white pepper, and dash salt. Cover and heat slowly just to boiling, stirring occasionally. Makes 6 servings.

New England Corn Chowder is flavored with bits of crisp-cooked bacon and onion. Serve with water biscuits, split, and toasted.

## Corn-Sausage Chowder

    1 pound bulk pork sausage
    1 small onion, thinly sliced
        (1/3 cup)
  1/3 cup chopped green pepper
    2 17-ounce cans cream-style corn
    1 12-ounce package loose-pack
        frozen hash brown potatoes
    3 cups water
    1 6-ounce can evaporated
        milk (2/3 cup)
    4 ounces sharp process American
        cheese, shredded (1 cup)

In large saucepan cook sausage with onion and green pepper till meat is browned and vegetables are crisp-tender. Drain off fat. Add corn, potatoes, water, evaporated milk, and 1/2 teaspoon salt. Heat to boiling. Reduce heat; simmer, covered, till potatoes are tender, about 15 minutes. Stir in cheese; heat till cheese melts. Serve immediately. Makes 8 to 10 servings.

## Swiss Corn Bake

    3 cups fresh corn cut from cob*
    1 6-ounce can evaporated
        milk (2/3 cup)
    1 beaten egg
    2 tablespoons finely chopped
        onion
  1/2 teaspoon salt
    4 ounces process Swiss cheese,
        shredded (1 cup)
  1/2 cup soft bread crumbs
    1 tablespoon butter or
        margarine, melted

Cook fresh corn in 1 cup boiling salted water for 2 to 3 minutes or just till tender; drain well. Combine corn, evaporated milk, egg, onion, salt, dash pepper, and 3/4 *cup* of the cheese. Turn into 10x6x1 1/2-inch baking dish.

    Toss bread crumbs with melted butter or margarine and the remaining 1/4 cup cheese. Sprinkle over corn mixture. Bake at 350° for 25 to 30 minutes. Garnish with green pepper rings, if desired. Makes 4 to 6 servings.

    * Or, use two 9-ounce packages frozen corn, cooked according to package directions and drained, *or* two 17-ounce cans whole kernel corn, drained, for the fresh cut corn.

## Corn O'Brien

    1 cup diced celery
  1/4 cup butter or margarine
    1 17-ounce can whole kernel corn,
        drained
  1/4 cup chopped canned pimiento
  3/4 teaspoon salt

In a saucepan combine celery and butter. Cook for 5 minutes. Add drained corn, pimiento, salt, and dash pepper. Cover; cook 10 minutes longer, stirring occasionally with a fork. Serve at once. Makes 6 to 8 servings.

## Creamy Corn

    1 3-ounce package cream cheese,
        softened
  1/4 cup milk
    1 tablespoon butter or margarine
  1/2 teaspoon onion salt
    1 17-ounce can whole kernel corn,
        drained

In saucepan combine cream cheese, milk, butter, and onion salt. Stir over low heat till cheese melts. Stir in corn; continue cooking until corn is heated through. Turn into serving dish. Trim with parsley or sprinkle with paprika, if desired. Makes 4 or 5 servings.

## Corn Curry

    3 tablespoons butter or margarine
 1 1/2 to 2 cups frozen or fresh corn
        cut from cob*
    2 tablespoons chopped green
        pepper
    2 tablespoons chopped onion
  1/4 to 1/2 teaspoon curry powder
  1/2 cup dairy sour cream

Melt butter in skillet. Add corn, green pepper, onion, and curry powder. Cover; cook over low heat till vegetables are just tender, 8 to 10 minutes. Stir in sour cream. Season with salt and pepper. Heat, stirring constantly. *Do not boil* the mixture. Makes 4 servings.

    * Or, use drained canned whole kernel corn or leftover corn cut off the cob. Add to cooked green pepper and onion with sour cream.

Spanish Corn Bread has double corn flavor. It starts with a corn muffin mix, then canned corn is added to the batter.

## Golden Corn Fry

*Good use for leftover corn-on-the-cob—*

> 2 tablespoons butter or margarine
> 3 cups frozen or fresh corn cut
>     from cob (4 to 6 medium ears)
> ½ cup light cream
> 2 tablespoons snipped chives
> 1 clove garlic, minced
>   Dash salt
>   Dash pepper
> ¼ cup shredded Parmesan cheese

Melt butter or margarine in saucepan. Add corn, cream, chives, garlic, salt, and pepper. Cover; simmer 10 to 15 minutes, stirring occasionally. Sprinkle with cheese. Remove from heat; let stand covered till cheese melts. Serve hot. Makes 4 to 6 servings.

*Corn products:* In addition to the fresh, frozen, and canned corn products, there are several other products made from corn. Cornstarch, corn syrup, corn oil, cornmeal, grits, popcorn, hominy, cereals, corn flour, animal feed, and laundry starch are all made with this most versatile crop. Corn is also used commercially in convenience mixes. (See also *Vegetable.*)

**CORN BREAD**—A quick bread made with cornmeal. It is one of the easiest breads to prepare and can be made simply with cornmeal, flour, eggs, milk, shortening, sugar, salt, and a leavening agent, such as baking powder. Some varieties are made without the flour, for example corn pone.

In addition to being a delicious hot bread to be eaten as is, corn bread can also be split and used as a base for creamed mixtures. Or, the corn bread batter can be baked atop a casserole. To achieve a different shape, bake the batter in corn stick pans for individual servings.

Corn bread can be purchased at some bakeries, or made at home from a mix or from simple ingredients. (See also *Bread.*)

## Spanish Corn Bread

> 1 14-ounce package corn muffin
>     mix
> ½ teaspoon dry mustard
>         • • •
> 1 12-ounce can whole kernel corn
>     with peppers, drained
> ¼ cup finely chopped onion
> 1 beaten egg
> ¾ cup milk

Combine corn muffin mix and dry mustard. Stir in corn, onion, egg, and milk; mix just till combined. Turn batter into greased 8x8x2-inch baking pan. Bake at 400° till done, about 30 minutes. Cut into squares and serve the bread while warm.

## Speedy Corn Bread Pie

*Keep ingredients on hand for a quick meal—*

> 2 15-ounce cans barbecue sauce
>     and beef
> 1 8-ounce can kidney beans,
>     drained
> 1 8-ounce package corn muffin mix

Combine first 2 ingredients; bring to boiling. Pour into 1½-quart casserole. Prepare corn muffin mix following package directions. Spread atop *hot* meat mixture. Bake at 400° for 20 to 25 minutes. Makes 6 servings.

## Perfect Corn Bread

1 cup sifted all-purpose flour
1/4 cup sugar
4 teaspoons baking powder
3/4 teaspoon salt
1 cup yellow cornmeal
2 eggs
1 cup milk
1/4 cup shortening

Sift flour with sugar, baking powder, and salt; stir in cornmeal. Add eggs, milk, and shortening. Beat with rotary or electric beater till just smooth. (Do not overbeat.) Pour into greased 9x9x2-inch pan. Bake at 425° till done, 20 to 25 minutes. Cut into squares.

*Corn Sticks:* Spoon batter into greased cornstick pans, filling 2/3 full. Bake at 425° for 12 to 15 minutes. Makes 18.

**CORN CHIP**—A crisp, waferlike snack made from corn. It is manufactured by cooking, soaking, and grinding white and yellow corn into a dough called *masa*. This dough is put through a press, forming its characteristic shape, then fried and salted before packaging in boxes or bags.

Other chips are made only from yellow corn. These types of chips are cut into shapes before being toasted and fried.

Corn chips make delightful snacks alone or with dips, and add special flavor and texture to prepared dishes.

## Zippy Ham Dip

Beat two 3-ounce packages cream cheese, softened, with 1/3 cup milk till light and creamy. Stir in 1 1/2 cups ground fully cooked ham; 2 tablespoons finely chopped green pepper; and 1 tablespoon prepared horseradish. Cover; chill thoroughly. Serve with corn chips as dippers. Makes 2 cups dip.

### *A hot salad*

←Taco Salad has all the ingredients of the familiar Mexican sandwich. For extra zip add a dash of bottled hot pepper sauce.

## Taco Salad

1 pound ground beef
1/2 envelope dry onion soup mix (1/4 cup)
3/4 cup water
. . .
1 medium head lettuce, torn in bite-size pieces (about 4 cups)
1 large tomato, cut in wedges
1 small onion, thinly sliced and separated in rings
1/4 cup chopped green pepper
1/2 cup sliced ripe olives
4 ounces sharp Cheddar cheese, shredded (1 cup)
1 6-ounce package corn chips

In skillet brown ground beef. Sprinkle onion soup mix over meat; stir in the water. Simmer, uncovered, 10 minutes. In salad bowl combine lettuce, tomato, onion, green pepper, olives, and cheese; toss well. Spoon on meat; top with corn chips. Makes 4 to 6 servings.

## Mexican-Style Casserole

5 pounds ground beef
4 medium onions, chopped (2 cups)
1 cup chopped green pepper
1 tablespoon chili powder
2 teaspoons dried oregano leaves, crushed
2 teaspoons salt
3 10 1/2-ounce cans tomato purée
2 28-ounce cans tomatoes, cut up
2 16-ounce cans red kidney beans, drained
5 cups crushed corn chips (about 6 ounces)
8 ounces process American cheese, shredded (2 cups)

Divide beef, onion, and green pepper between 2 large skillets. Cook till meat is browned and vegetables are tender; drain off excess fat. Divide next 6 ingredients and *4 cups* of the chips between the 2 skillets; mix. Simmer, uncovered, for 5 minutes. Turn into *two* 13x9x2-inch baking dishes. Bake, uncovered, at 350° till hot, about 35 minutes. Sprinkle remaining corn chips and cheese atop casseroles. Bake 5 minutes longer. Makes 24 servings.

**CORNED**—The process of preserving foods in a salt brine solution or with coarse salt. It was originally used as a method of storing meat without refrigeration.

**CORNED BEEF**—The brisket, plate, or round of beef cured or pickled in a strong salt brine. All bones and extra fat are removed from the cut of meat before it is cured. The brine can either be pumped into the meat or the meat can be soaked in the brine. Other ingredients in the brine include sugar, which adds flavor, and salts called nitrates and nitrites, which affect the color of the meat. Some corned beef is grayish brown in color because nitrates were not used in the processing. Other pieces of corned beef are dark red due to the action of the nitrates. Unlike other meats that are cured, for example, ham or picnic, corned beef is not smoked.

Corned beef can be purchased with either a mild cure or a cure including spices. The spices, such as allspice, cloves, and peppercorns, and herbs, including bay leaves, are added for additional flavor. Garlic can also be added.

Corned beef contains protein and some of the B vitamins, thiamine, riboflavin, and niacin; however, thiamine is partially destroyed when the meat is cured.

Store ready-to-cook corned beef as it comes from the grocery store in its original wrapper. Place it in the refrigerator and for best eating quality, do not store for longer than a week. Freezing corned beef is not recommended for best quality.

Because it is made from less tender cuts of beef, corned beef needs long, slow cooking in liquid. Some corned beef has been made tender during processing. This pretenderized meat can be roasted in the oven following label directions.

Typical dishes made with corned beef are corned beef and cabbage and corned beef hash. It also makes delicious sandwiches and is used in familiar Reuben sandwiches with sauerkraut and cheese.

Corned beef not only can be purchased at the meat counter ready to cook, but it is also available canned, fully cooked. Canned corned beef hash and corned beef luncheon meat are also products that can be obtained in food stores.

## Corned Beef with Sweets

1 3- or 4-pound ready-to-cook
   corned beef brisket
½ cup chopped onion
8 sweet potatoes, peeled
2 10-ounce packages frozen
   Brussels sprouts

Place corned beef brisket in Dutch oven and barely cover with water. Add onion. If seasonings are not in package, add 2 bay leaves, and 6 whole black peppercorns. Cover; simmer till almost tender, about 2½ to 3 hours.

Add sweet potatoes and cook 30 minutes more. Add frozen Brussels sprouts and cook 15 minutes longer. Remove bay leaves and serve vegetables with meat. Makes 8 servings.

## Peach-Glazed Corned Beef

1 3-pound ready-to-cook corned
   beef brisket
1 29-ounce can peach halves
¼ cup brown sugar
¼ cup catsup
2 tablespoons vinegar
2 teaspoons prepared mustard

Place corned beef brisket in Dutch oven; add water to cover. If seasonings are not in package, add 1 bay leaf. Cover and simmer till meat is tender, about 2½ to 3 hours. Remove from heat; cool meat in cooking liquid. Remove meat; slice across the grain.

Arrange slices, overlapping, in 12x7½x2-inch baking dish. Drain peaches, reserving ¼ cup syrup. Arrange peaches around meat. Combine reserved syrup and remaining ingredients. Pour over meat. Bake at 350° for 1 hour, basting with the sauce occasionally. Serves 6.

## Grilled Reubens

Spread 6 slices pumpernickel or rye bread with ½ cup Thousand Island salad dressing. Top each with 1 slice Swiss cheese, 2 tablespoons well-drained sauerkraut, thin slices cooked or canned corned beef, and a second bread slice. Butter tops and bottoms of sandwiches. Grill on both sides till hot and cheese melts. Serve hot. Makes 6 sandwiches.

## Reuben Roll-Ups

  1 **package refrigerated crescent
      rolls (8 rolls)**
  1 **8-ounce can sauerkraut, well
      drained**
  1 **tablespoon Thousand Island salad
      dressing**
  8 **thin slices cooked corned
      beef (about 4 ounces)**
  2 **slices process Swiss cheese, cut
      in ½-inch strips**

Unroll crescent roll dough; separate into 8 triangles. Snip drained sauerkraut in can to cut long strands; combine with salad dressing. Place one slice corned beef across wide end of triangle. Spread 2 tablespoons sauerkraut on corned beef. Top with 2 strips of cheese. Roll up, beginning at wide end of triangle. Bake on *ungreased* baking sheet at 375° till golden brown, about 10 to 15 minutes. Serve the roll-ups hot. Makes 8 servings.

Canned corned beef products make delicious and quick additions to a countless number of main dish items—from molded salads to casseroles and skillet dishes—perfect for supper. (See also *Beef.*)

For tender slices, carve corned beef brisket across grain at a slight angle, making slices ⅛ to ¼ inch thick. Carve from two sides, alternating sides for equal pieces.

## Corned Beef Loaf

*A main-dish salad—*

In saucepan soften 2 envelopes unflavored gelatin in 1 cup tomato juice; stir over low heat till gelatin is dissolved. Add 1 cup tomato juice, 1 cup mayonnaise, 2 teaspoons lemon juice, and ½ teaspoon salt. Beat smooth with rotary beater. Chill till partially set.

Fold in one 12-ounce can corned beef, crumbled (2 cups); ½ cup chopped celery; ½ cup chopped unpeeled cucumber; and 1 tablespoon chopped onion into gelatin mixture. Pour into an 8½x4½x2½-inch loaf dish. Chill till firm. Unmold onto a platter lined with salad greens. Makes 4 to 6 servings.

## Corned Beef and Noodles

Cook 4 ounces medium noodles (2 cups) according to package directions; drain. In saucepan melt 3 tablespoons butter or margarine; stir in 3 tablespoons all-purpose flour. Add 2¼ cups milk; cook quickly, stirring constantly, till mixture thickens and bubbles. Stir in 1 tablespoon prepared horseradish, 2 teaspoons salt, 1 teaspoon prepared mustard, and dash pepper; mix thoroughly.

Add one 10-ounce package frozen peas, thawed, and noodles. Turn into 10x6x1½-inch baking dish. Arrange one 12-ounce can corned beef, cut in 6 slices, over noodles. Bake at 350° for 30 minutes. Makes 5 or 6 servings.

## Jazzy Hash

  1 **15-ounce can corned beef hash**
  ½ **cup dairy sour cream**
  ¼ **cup red Burgundy**
  2 **beaten eggs**
  2 **tablespoons chopped onion**
  1 **small clove garlic, minced**
  1 **cup soft bread crumbs**
  1 **tablespoon butter, melted
      Dash paprika**

Combine first 6 ingredients and dash pepper; mix well. Spoon into 4 individual casseroles or one 8-inch pie plate. Combine remaining ingredients; sprinkle over hash. Bake at 350° for 25 to 30 minutes. Makes 4 servings.

## Corned Beef Bake

    1 12-ounce can corned beef, finely
         chopped
    ½ cup finely chopped green pepper
    ½ cup finely chopped onion
    ½ cup mayonnaise
         Dash pepper
    1 beaten egg
    ½ cup fine dry bread crumbs
    2 tablespoons shortening
    3 slices sharp process American
         cheese
    1 10½-ounce can condensed cream
         of celery soup
    1 8¼-ounce can mixed vegetables,
         drained
    ⅓ cup milk
    3 large English muffins, halved
         and toasted

Combine corned beef, green pepper, onion, mayonnaise, and pepper. Shape into 6 patties. Blend egg and 1 tablespoon water; dip patties into egg, then crumbs. Brown lightly in hot shortening. Place patties in 10x6x1½-inch baking dish. Quarter cheese slices diagonally; overlap 2 triangles atop each patty. Combine soup, vegetables, and milk; heat. Pour around patties. Bake at 350° till hot, about 12 minutes. Serve on muffins. Makes 6 servings.

## Corned Beef Pie

*Made in a jiffy with corned beef hash—*

    1 15-ounce can corned beef hash
    ¼ cup catsup
    1 slightly beaten egg
              • • •
    1 10-ounce package frozen baby
         limas
    2 ounces process American cheese,
         shredded (½ cup)
    2 tablespoons milk

### *Quick-cooking main dish*

←A well-flavored corned beef patty served atop a toasted English muffin makes Corned Beef Bake hearty enough for any supper.

Combine the hash, catsup, and egg in a bowl. Spread corned beef mixture on bottom and sides of greased 8-inch pie plate. Bake at 350° for about 30 minutes.

Meanwhile, cook limas according to package directions; drain thoroughly. Fill corned beef crust with limas. Combine shredded cheese and milk in a saucepan. Heat over *very low heat*, stirring constantly, till cheese melts. Pour cheese sauce over limas. Cut into wedges to serve. Makes 4 or 5 servings.

**CORNET**—1. A name for the cone-shaped thin, waferlike pastry that is usually filled with a cream mixture. 2. A piece of paper or a thin slice of meat rolled into a cone shape. The paper cones can be used as decorating tubes. Sometimes the pastry cones are referred to as cornucopias.

**CORNFLAKES**—A crisp, ready-to-eat cereal made from milled corn. In the processing, sugar, salt, and malt flavoring are combined with the corn. The mixture is cooked and then rolled into flakes under many tons of pressure. At this point, the flakes are toasted at a high temperature for a very short period of time.

During processing, the cornflakes are restored to the whole corn nutritive levels. One cup of cornflakes adds about 95 calories to the diet, plus some sodium, the B vitamin, thiamine, and carbohydrates.

Cornflakes can be purchased in several package sizes, either plain or presweetened with a sugar coating. Another cornflake product that is available is the ready-to-use cornflake crumbs. They can be incorporated into meatballs, quick breads, pancakes, and desserts, or used as a coating for chicken or chops. (See also *Cereal*.)

**CORN FLOUR**—Cornmeal that is ground and sieved until it resembles wheat flour. Corn flour in English cookery is called cornstarch. (See also *Flour*.)

**CORNISH GAME HEN**—The smallest, youngest member of the chicken family, sometimes referred to as Rock Cornish Hen.

It was developed as a crossbreed between the English Cornish male chicken and the White Rock female chicken. This breed of chicken is fed for four weeks and at this time certain females are selected and put on a high-fat diet for an additional two weeks. They usually weigh 1½ pounds or less when marketed and have a small bone structure, but they are well fleshed. The meat from the Cornish game hen is light and has a delicate flavor very much like the white meat of chicken.

Cornish game hens are available year-round in the frozen food department in the supermarket. Store in the freezer, then thaw wrapped birds before cooking, either in the refrigerator or in cold water, changing the water often.

Since the bird is so young and tender, it can be roasted, broiled, or fried and is delightful when stuffed before roasting. Most often a small bird makes one generous individual serving. (See also *Chicken*.)

## Rice-Stuffed Cornish Game Hens

> 2 1-pound ready-to-cook Cornish game hens
> 2 tablespoons slivered almonds
> 2 tablespoons finely chopped onion
> ⅓ cup uncooked long-grain rice
> 3 tablespoons butter or margarine
> 1 cup water
> 1 chicken bouillon cube
> 1 teaspoon lemon juice
> ½ teaspoon salt
> 1 3-ounce can chopped mushrooms, drained (½ cup)
> Butter or margarine, melted

Season game hens inside and out with salt and pepper. In small saucepan cook almonds, onion, and rice in 3 tablespoons butter for 5 to 10 minutes, stirring frequently.

Add water, bouillon cube, lemon juice, and ½ teaspoon salt. Bring mixture to boiling, stirring to dissolve bouillon cube. Reduce heat; cover and cook slowly till liquid is absorbed and rice is fluffy, about 20 to 25 minutes. Stir in drained mushrooms.

Lightly stuff birds with rice mixture. Follow directions for cooking according to How to Roast Cornish Game Hens chart (see page 648). Brush with melted butter or margarine before roasting and during last 15 minutes of roasting. Makes 2 servings.

## Cornish Hens Supreme

> 4 1- to 1½-pound ready-to-cook Cornish game hens
> ¼ cup butter or margarine, melted
>       • • •
> ⅓ cup sugar
> 1 17-ounce can fruit cocktail, drained (reserve syrup)
> ½ cup dry sauterne
> 2 tablespoons cornstarch
> ½ teaspoon salt
> ½ teaspoon grated orange peel
> ½ teaspoon grated lemon peel
> ¼ cup lemon juice

Salt inside of birds and truss. Follow directions for cooking according to How to Roast Cornish Game Hens chart (see page 648). Uncover and baste with melted butter or margarine the last hour of roasting. Serve with hot Wine Fruit Sauce. Makes 4 servings.

Wine Fruit Sauce: Caramelize sugar over low heat in heavy saucepan. Heat fruit cocktail syrup to boiling; slowly add to melted sugar. Cook and stir till dissolved. Combine wine, cornstarch, salt, and grated peels. Stir into hot syrup mixture and cook, stirring constantly, until mixture thickens and bubbles. Add lemon juice and drained fruit cocktail. Heat just to boiling. Makes 2 cups.

## Grill-Broiled Cornish Game Hens

Split four 1-pound ready-to-cook Cornish game hens in half lengthwise. Season. Broil slowly, bone side down, over *medium* coals, brushing well with melted butter.

When bone side is well browned, about 20 minutes, turn skin side down. Broil till tender, about 20 to 25 minutes longer. For glaze, brush both sides with a mixture of ¼ cup canned condensed consommé and ¼ cup light corn syrup. Broil 1 or 2 minutes longer to glaze Cornish hens. Makes 4 servings.

## *A candlelight dinner for two*

Cooked whole cranberries spooned into hollowed-out lemon cups makes the ideal trim for Rice-Stuffed Cornish Game Hens.

### How to roast cornish game hens

Rinse bird; dry. Salt cavity; stuff, if desired. Close opening with skewers; lace. Place breast up on rack in shallow pan. Brush with salad oil. Roast loosely covered 30 minutes. Uncover; roast till done, 1 hour more.

Ready-to-cook weight
1 to 1½ pounds

Oven temperature
375°

Total roasting time
1½ hours

If desired, baste occasionally with melted butter or a glaze the last hour of roasting. To test for doneness, twist drumstick. It can be twisted easily in socket when done.

## Cornish Hens Burgundy

For stuffing, cook 3 tablespoons sliced green onion and tops in 2 tablespoons butter till tender. Remove from heat and stir in ¼ cup toasted slivered almonds, 3 tablespoons snipped parsley, ⅛ teaspoon salt, and dash pepper. Add ½ cup cooked long-grain rice. Toss.

Salt, lightly stuff, then truss two 1- to 1½-pound ready-to-cook Cornish game hens. Follow directions for cooking according to How to Roast Cornish Game Hens chart (see above). Uncover and baste often with Burgundy Glaze the last hour of roasting. Makes 2 servings.

*Burgundy Glaze:* Combine in a saucepan ½ cup red Burgundy, ½ cup currant jelly, 2 tablespoons butter, 1 tablespoon lemon juice, 2 teaspoons cornstarch, 2 teaspoons Worcestershire sauce, ½ teaspoon ground allspice, dash salt, and dash pepper. Cook till mixture thickens and bubbles. Use to glaze bird during roasting; pass remaining as sauce.

## Broiled Cornish Game Hens

Split one 1- to 1½-pound ready-to-cook Cornish game hen in half lengthwise. Place skin side down in broiler pan (no rack).

Brush with melted butter or margarine. Season with salt and pepper. Broil 7 inches from heat for 15 minutes. Brush occasionally with melted butter. Turn; broil till done, about 15 minutes longer. Makes 2 servings.

**CORNISH PASTY**—A main dish turnover filled with seasoned ground meat or meat cubes and various vegetables. One of the vegetables most often included in the flaky, pastrylike crust is potatoes.

The pasty is baked in the oven and can be eaten with the fingers, either hot or cold. This particular pasty derives its name from the town in England, named Cornwall, where it originated.

**CORNMEAL**—White or yellow corn that has been ground into a meal.

In modern day processing, cornmeal is made from mechanically hulled and almost completely degerminated corn. The corn is ground between heavy steel rollers to fine granules, then sieved or bolted. The medium-sized granules are called grits, the finer ones are cornmeal, and the finest granules are called corn flour. Cornmeal made by this process feels dry and granular. It will keep well because most of the germ has been removed and it can be stored, tightly covered, on the shelf in a cool, dry place.

Another processing method is stone-ground cornmeal. White or yellow corn is ground in the old-fashioned way, between stones. Sometimes it is called water-ground cornmeal. This name is a carry-over from the days when grinding stones were turned by waterpower. With this process the hull and germ are not removed, although a small amount of the hull may be sieved out of the ground corn. It feels soft to the touch and is considered by some to have a true corn flavor. Stone-ground cornmeal does not keep as well and should be stored on the refrigerator shelf because it has a higher fat content.

Some cornmeal products that are available are enriched even to the point that they contain more nutrients than the whole corn. The B vitamins, thiamine, niacin, and riboflavin are added. Yellow cornmeal also contains some vitamin A.

Cornmeal is used in various countries in typical dishes, such as *polenta*, which is mush in Italian. In America, it is used to make breads, muffins, mush, and toppings for casseroles. (See *Corn Bread, Corn Stick, Indian Pudding, Mush, Scrapple* for additional information.)

## Yankee Bacon Bake

½ pound sliced bacon
½ cup cornmeal
2 cups milk
½ cup sifted all-purpose flour
1 tablespoon sugar
1 teaspoon baking powder
½ teaspoon salt
3 well-beaten egg yolks
3 stiffly beaten egg whites

Quarter bacon slices. Cook till crisp; drain. Mix cornmeal with 1 *cup* of the milk. Cook till thickened; remove from heat. Sift together flour, sugar, baking powder, and salt; blend into cornmeal. Mix in remaining milk and egg yolks; fold in egg whites and crisp-cooked bacon. Bake in greased 2-quart casserole at 325° about 1 hour. Makes 6 servings.

**CORN MUFFIN**—A simple, quick bread made with cornmeal and baked in individual portions. Sometimes this muffin is referred to as a cornmeal muffin.

Variations of corn muffins can be made by adding a few ingredients. Crumbled, cooked bacon or canned corn can be added to the batter before turning into muffin cups. Or, other flavors, such as molasses, can be incorporated into the batter.

To make preparation of these muffins even easier, there are several simple-to-prepare mixes available. These mixes can also be used as a recipe ingredient, such as in main dish toppers. (See also *Muffin.*)

## Bacon-Chive Corn Muffins

1 14-ounce package corn muffin mix
2 teaspoons snipped chives
6 slices bacon, crisp-cooked, drained, and crumbled

Prepare muffin mix according to package directions. Fold in chives, dash pepper, and bacon. Turn into 12 greased 2¾-inch muffin pans and bake at 400° till done, 15 to 17 minutes. Serve hot. Makes 12 muffins.

## Molasses Corn Muffins

½ cup shortening
½ cup sugar
2 eggs
½ cup molasses
1 cup milk
1 cup sifted all-purpose flour
3 teaspoons baking powder
½ teaspoon salt
½ cup yellow cornmeal
1½ cups whole bran

Cream shortening and sugar. Beat in eggs, one at a time. Stir in molasses and milk. Sift together flour, baking powder, and salt; stir in cornmeal and bran. Add to creamed mixture, stirring just till blended. Fill paper bake cups in muffin pans ⅔ full. Bake at 375° till done, 22 to 24 minutes. Makes 18.

## Sausage-Muffin Bake

1 pound bulk pork sausage
1 16-ounce can whole cranberry sauce
1 medium orange, peeled and cut up
1 8-ounce package corn muffin mix

Brown sausage, breaking up into small pieces; drain. Spread meat in 8x8x2-inch baking dish. Top with cranberry, then with orange. Prepare muffin mix following package directions. Pour over fruit; spread to edges. Bake at 375° for 35 to 40 minutes. Makes 6 servings.

**CORN OIL**—A golden yellow oil extracted from the germ of the corn kernel. It is odorless and flavorless, making it useful either as a salad or cooking oil. Corn oil has a high smoke point (the temperature at which fat breaks down), so it is excellent for deep-fat frying and fondue cookery. It is used in manufacturing some margarines. (See *Fat, Oil* for additional information.)

**CORN OYSTER**—A fritter made with corn, cooked on a griddle. (See also *Fritter*.)

**CORN PONE**—A type of plain, unsweetened, corn bread usually made in oval or stick-like shapes. Originally they were made by the Indians who baked them in the ashes of a fire and called them *apones*. Early settlers, however, changed the name and cooked them over the fire. Now, they are most popular in the South.

**CORN POPPER**—1. A long-handled utensil made of wire used for popping corn over direct heat. 2. An electric appliance with a base containing the heating element, a pan for the fat and corn, and a cover.

**CORN PUDDING**—A custardy vegetable mixture made with fresh or canned corn that is tested for doneness like a baked custard.

## Corn Pudding

    3 **slightly beaten eggs**
    2 **cups drained cooked or canned**
       **whole kernel corn**
    2 **cups milk, scalded**
    ⅓ **cup finely chopped onion**
    1 **tablespoon butter, melted**
    1 **teaspoon sugar**

Combine eggs, corn, milk, onion, butter, sugar, and 1 teaspoon salt. Pour into greased 1½-quart casserole. Set dish in shallow pan. Fill pan to 1 inch with hot water. Bake at 350° till knife inserted halfway between center and edge comes out clean, about 40 to 45 minutes. Let stand 10 minutes at room temperature before serving. Makes 6 servings.

## Quick Corn Pudding

Combine one 17-ounce can cream-style corn and one 10½-ounce can condensed cream of chicken soup. Stir in 3 well-beaten eggs. Add 1 tablespoon instant minced onion and dash pepper. Pour into a 1½-quart casserole. Set dish in shallow pan. Fill pan to 1 inch with hot water. Bake at 325° till knife inserted halfway between center and edge comes out clean, about 1¼ hours. Makes 6 servings.

**CORN RELISH**—A tangy side dish made with corn and served as a meat or main dish accompaniment. It often includes other vegetables and may be thickened slightly. Sometimes corn relish has a sweet-sour flavor. (See also *Relish*.)

## Corn Relish

    ⅓ **cup sugar**
    1 **tablespoon cornstarch**
    1 **teaspoon instant minced onion**
    1 **teaspoon turmeric**
    ½ **teaspoon celery seed**
    ¼ **cup vinegar**
    1 **12-ounce can whole kernel corn**
    2 **tablespoons finely chopped**
       **green pepper**
    1 **tablespoon finely chopped**
       **canned pimiento**

In saucepan combine first 7 ingredients and ¼ cup water. Cook and stir till mixture thickens and bubbles. Stir in the green pepper and pimiento. Chill. Makes 1¾ cups.

Peppy Corn Relish adds a colorful note to any relish tray and especially sparks the flavor of grilled franks or hamburgers.

**CORNSTARCH** – A white, powdery substance refined from corn and used as a thickener for puddings, sauces, pie fillings, and gravies. When cornstarch is used, the thickened product has a more translucent appearance than when it is thickened with flour. Cornstarch in a reduced amount can be substituted for the flour used to thicken some sauces and gravies. The substitution is one tablespoon cornstarch equals two tablespoons flour.

When cooking with cornstarch, clumping in hot liquids can be prevented by mixing the cornstarch with sugar or a little cold liquid before adding it to the hot mixture. A cornstarch-thickened mixture should be stirred constantly until it begins to thicken. Then it should be stirred as little as possible and cooked long enough for the raw starch flavor to disappear and the mixture to take on a clear appearance. The mixture should not be overcooked.

Acids such as vinegar or lemon juice affect the thickness of the mixture and should be added after the cornstarch is completely cooked and removed from heat.

**CORN STICK** – A corn bread-type mixture that is baked in special heavy metal pans which are shaped like ears of corn.

## Double Corn Sticks

In a bowl sift together 1 cup sifted all-purpose flour, 2 tablespoons sugar, 2 teaspoons baking powder, and ¾ teaspoon salt. Stir in 1 cup yellow cornmeal till blended.

Blend 1 well-beaten egg, one 8¾-ounce can cream-style corn, ¾ cup milk, and 2 tablespoons salad oil. Add to dry ingredients and stir just till moistened.

Preheat corn-stick pans in oven, then grease generously. Fill pans ⅔ full. Bake at 425° for about 20 minutes. Makes about 18 corn sticks.

**CORN SUGAR** – A granulated sugar derived from cornstarch which is broken down by acids or enzymes into sugar, then purified and dried. It is also referred to as glucose and has less sweetening power than regular sugar. (See also *Sugar.*)

Bake a batch of Double Corn Sticks for lunch or supper and serve them with a spicy, chili-type mixture—better have plenty for seconds! Next time, try corn sticks from a mix.

**CORN SYRUP**—A thick, clear, sweet liquid made by converting cornstarch into syrup. Corn syrups vary in color from a light crystal-clear to dark. The darkest color indicates the strongest flavor.

Corn syrup is a carbohydrate; therefore, it supplies energy for the body's activities. A tablespoon of corn syrup contains approximately 60 calories.

Both light and dark corn syrup can be purchased in pint and quart containers. At home, store these on the cabinet shelf; just be sure the cap is screwed on securely.

There are many uses for corn syrup as a topping and as an ingredient in recipes. As a topping, it goes well with pancakes, waffles, French toast, and ice cream. Sometimes, corn syrup mixtures are poured over buns and sweet rolls for a topping, adding texture and flavor.

When used as an ingredient, corn syrup gives food body, a shiny appearance, and flavor. Several characteristics of corn syrup make it especially good to use in candy. The syrup is not as sweet as granulated sugar; therefore, the candy does not become overly sweet. And because the syrup does not crystallize as easily as sugar, it helps to control the reaction of the ingredients in candy making—fudge can be made creamy and smooth, taffy soft and chewy, and brittles crisp and nonsticky.

Other examples of foods commonly made with corn syrup are pies, baby formulas, punches, and jams. (See also *Syrup.*)

## Butterscotch Swirls

    1 package active dry yeast
2¼ to 2¾ cups sifted all-purpose
        flour
    ¾ cup milk
    ½ cup sugar
    ¼ cup shortening
          • • •
    2 tablespoons butter or margarine,
        softened
    ½ teaspoon ground cinnamon
    1 6-ounce package butterscotch
        pieces
    ¼ cup light corn syrup
    2 tablespoons butter or margarine
    ½ cup chopped walnuts

In large mixer bowl, combine active dry yeast and 1¼ *cups* flour. Heat milk, ¼ *cup* sugar, shortening, and 1 teaspoon salt just till warm, stirring occasionally to melt shortening. Add to dry mixture in bowl. Beat at low speed with electric mixer for ½ minute, scraping sides of bowl constantly. Beat 3 minutes at high speed. By hand stir in enough of the remaining flour to make a soft dough. On lightly floured surface, knead 8 to 10 minutes. Place in greased bowl, turning once to grease surface. Cover; let double in warm place (about 1½ hours). Punch down; let rest 10 minutes.

Roll to 16x8-inch rectangle. Spread with the 2 tablespoons soft butter. Mix the remaining sugar and cinnamon; sprinkle over buttered rectangle. Roll lengthwise; seal. Cut in 1-inch slices. Place cut side down on greased 9x9x2-inch baking pan. Drizzle with Butterscotch Topping. Cover rolls; let double, about 40 minutes. Bake at 350° till done, about 30 minutes. Cool 2 to 3 minutes; invert on board.

*Butterscotch Topping:* Combine butterscotch pieces, corn syrup, the 2 tablespoons butter, and 2 tablespoons water. Melt over low heat, stirring occasionally. Cool. Add nuts.

**CORNUCOPIA** (*kôr′ nuh ko′ pe uh*)—A container shaped like a horn or cone. A cornucopia made of pastry and filled with whipped cream makes an unusual dessert.

**COS LETTUCE**—Another name for romaine. (See also *Romaine.*)

**COSTMARY** (*kost′ mâr′ ē*)—An herb with a sweet, minty, or lemony fragrance and a bitter, lemony flavor. The plant grows to three feet in height, has daisylike flowers, and long, slender, green leaves.

Formerly, costmary had many diversified uses. In the Middle Ages, it was used to flavor ales and beers; thus, the name alecost was also given to the herb. The long, slender leaf has been popular as a bookmarker and for perfuming linens.

Today, costmary is used in salads and for flavoring. It adds a minty, lemony flavor to meats, peas, potatoes, beverages, and stuffings. (See also *Herb.*)

**CÔTELETTE** (*kōt let′*)—A French term meaning chop or cutlet.